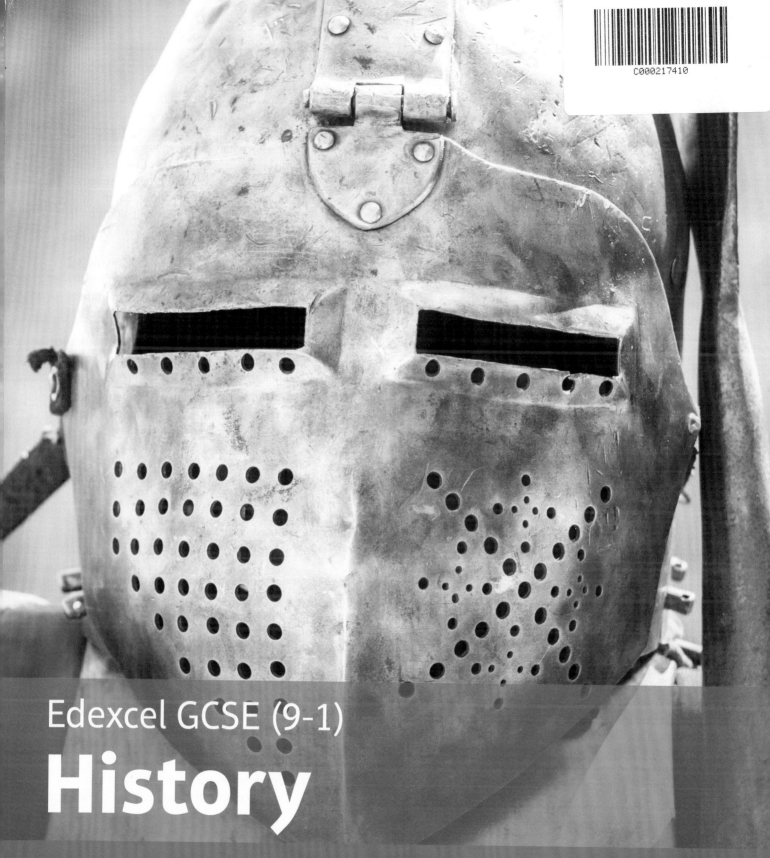

Edexcel GCSE (9-1)
History

The reigns of King Richard I and King John, 1189–1216

Series Editor: Angela Leonard   Author: Sarah Moffatt

PEARSON

Published by Pearson Education Limited, 80 Strand, London, WC2R 0RL.

www.pearsonschoolsandfecolleges.co.uk

Copies of official specifications for all Edexcel qualifications may be found on the website: www.edexcel.com

Text © Pearson Education Limited 2016

Series editor: Angela Leonard
Designed by Colin Tilley Loughrey, Pearson Education Limited
Typeset by Phoenix Photosetting, Chatham, Kent
Original illustrations © Pearson Education Limited
Illustrated by KJA Artists Illustration Agency and Phoenix Photosetting, Chatham, Kent.

Cover design by Colin Tilley Loughrey
Picture research by Christine Martin
Cover photo © Alamy Images: Ryhor Bruyeu

The right of Sarah Moffatt to be identified as author of this work has been asserted by her in accordance with the Copyright, Designs and Patents Act 1988.

First published 2016

19 18 17 16
10 9 8 7 6 5 4 3 2

British Library Cataloguing in Publication Data
A catalogue record for this book is available from the British Library.
ISBN 978 1 292 12724 8

Printed in Slovakia by Neografia

A note from the publisher
In order to ensure that this resource offers high-quality support for the associated Pearson qualification, it has been through a review process by the awarding body. This process confirms that this resource fully covers the teaching and learning content of the specification or part of a specification at which it is aimed. It also confirms that it demonstrates an appropriate balance between the development of subject skills, knowledge and understanding, in addition to preparation for assessment.

Endorsement does not cover any guidance on assessment activities or processes (e.g. practice questions or advice on how to answer assessment questions), included in the resource nor does it prescribe any particular approach to the teaching or delivery of a related course.

While the publishers have made every attempt to ensure that advice on the qualification and its assessment is accurate, the official specification and associated assessment guidance materials are the only authoritative source of information and should always be referred to for definitive guidance.

Pearson examiners have not contributed to any sections in this resource relevant to examination papers for which they have responsibility.

Examiners will not use endorsed resources as a source of material for any assessment set by Pearson.

Endorsement of a resource does not mean that the resource is required to achieve this Pearson qualification, nor does it mean that it is the only suitable material available to support the qualification, and any resource lists produced by the awarding body shall include this and other appropriate resources.

Websites
Pearson Education Limited is not responsible for the content of any external internet sites. It is essential for tutors to preview each website before using it in class so as to ensure that the URL is still accurate, relevant and appropriate. We suggest that tutors bookmark useful websites and consider enabling students to access them through the school/college intranet.

Contents

How to use this book

What's covered?

This book covers the British Depth study on the reigns of King Richard I and King John, 1189–1216. This unit makes up 20% of your GCSE course, and will be examined in Paper 2.

Depth studies cover a short period of time, and require you to know about society, people and events in detail. You need to understand how the different aspects of the period fit together and affect each other. This book also explains the different types of exam questions you will need to answer, and includes advice and example answers to help you improve.

Features

As well as a clear, detailed explanation of the key knowledge you will need, you will also find a number of features in the book:

Key terms

Where you see a word followed by an asterisk, like this: Ransom*, you will be able to find a Key Terms box on that page that explains what the word means.

> **Key term**
>
> **Ransom***
>
> A payment demanded for the release of a prisoner. During wars, knights, barons and even kings were often captured, instead of killed, so that large ransoms could be demanded.

Activities

Every few pages, you'll find a box containing some activities designed to help check and embed knowledge and get you to really think about what you've studied. The activities start simple, but might get more challenging as you work through them.

Summaries and Checkpoints

At the end of each chunk of learning, the main points are summarised in a series of bullet points – great for embedding the core knowledge, and handy for revision.

Checkpoints help you to check and reflect on your learning. The Strengthen section helps you to consolidate knowledge and understanding, and check that you've grasped the basic ideas and skills. The Challenge questions push you to go beyond just understanding the information, and into evaluation and analysis of what you've studied.

Sources and Interpretations

Although source work and interpretations do not appear in Paper 2, you'll still find interesting contemporary material throughout the books, showing what people from the period said, thought or created, helping you to build your understanding of people in the past.

The book also includes extracts from the work of historians, showing how experts have interpreted the events you've been studying.

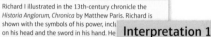

> **Source A**
>
> Richard I illustrated in the 13th-century chronicle the *Historia Anglorum, Chronica* by Matthew Paris. Richard is shown with the symbols of his power, inclu[ding] on his head and the sword in his hand. He [holds] one hand to show his close relationship wi[th]

> **Interpretation 1**
>
> David Starkey comments on John's style of ruling in *Crown and Country: A History of England Through Monarchy* (2010).
>
> John's obsession for record-keeping was a sign not of strength, but of weakness. He was so keen on documentation because he was so mistrustful of his subjects, and his subjects in turn distrusted a king who was always nit-picking and always eager to revive an old, outdated royal imposition or invent a new one. The result was tax, tax and more tax.

Extend your knowledge

These features contain useful additional information that adds depth to your knowledge, and to your answers. The information is closely related to the key issues in the unit, and questions are sometimes included, helping you to link the new details to the main content.

> **Extend your knowledge**
>
> **Household knights**
>
> There was also another group of knights: household knights. They did not hold land from their lord, instead they were maintained by the lord as a member of his household and he provided all their food and accommodation. The king had to keep a careful watch on the number of household knights that a baron kept. If it was very large, it might mean that the baron was keeping a private army. This could be a threat to the king if the baron decided to rebel.

Exam-style questions and tips

The book also includes extra exam-style questions you can use to practise. These appear in the chapters and are accompanied by a tip to help you get started on an answer.

Recap pages

At the end of each chapter, you'll find a page designed to help you to consolidate and reflect on the chapter as a whole. Each recap page includes a recall quiz, ideal for quickly checking your knowledge or for revision. Recap pages also include activities designed to help you summarise and analyse what you've learned, and also reflect on how each chapter links to other parts of the unit.

THINKING HISTORICALLY

These activities are designed to help you develop a better understanding of how history is constructed, and are focused on the key areas of Evidence, Interpretations, Cause & Consequence and Change & Continuity. In the British Depth Study, you will come across activities on Cause & Consequence, as this is a key focus for this unit.

The Thinking Historically approach has been developed in conjunction with Dr Arthur Chapman and the Institute of Education, UCL. It is based on research into the misconceptions that can hold students back in history.

THINKING HISTORICALLY ▶ Cause and Consequence (3c&d) — conceptual map reference

The Thinking Historically conceptual map can be found at: www.pearsonschools.co.uk/thinkinghistoricallygcse

WRITING HISTORICALLY

At the end of most chapters is a spread dedicated to helping you improve your writing skills. These include simple techniques you can use in your writing to make your answers clearer, more precise and better focused on the question you're answering.

The Writing Historically approach is based on the *Grammar for Writing* pedagogy developed by a team at the University of Exeter and popular in many English departments. Each spread uses examples from the preceding chapter, so it's relevant to what you've just been studying.

Preparing for your exams

At the back of the book, you'll find a special section dedicated to explaining and exemplifying the new Edexcel GCSE History exams. Advice on the demands of this paper, written by Angela Leonard, helps you prepare for and approach the exam with confidence. Each question type is explained through annotated sample answers at two levels, showing clearly how answers can be improved.

Pearson Progression Scale: This icon indicates the Step that a sample answer has been graded at on the Pearson Progression Scale.

This book is also available as an online ActiveBook, which can be licensed for your whole institution.

There is also an ActiveLearn Digital Service available to support delivery of this book, featuring a front-of-class version of the book, lesson plans, worksheets, exam practice PowerPoints, assessments, notes on Thinking Historically and Writing Historically, and more.

ActiveLearn
Digital Service

Timeline: The reigns of Richard I and King John

Events at home

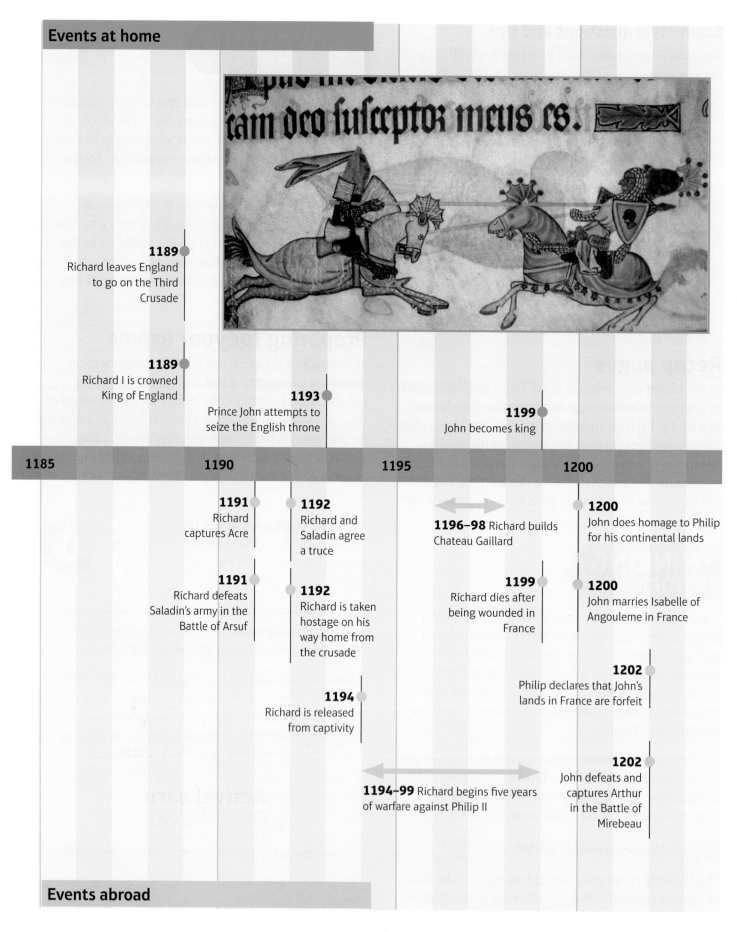

1189
Richard leaves England to go on the Third Crusade

1189
Richard I is crowned King of England

1193
Prince John attempts to seize the English throne

1199
John becomes king

| 1185 | 1190 | 1195 | 1200 |

1191
Richard captures Acre

1192
Richard and Saladin agree a truce

1196–98 Richard builds Chateau Gaillard

1200
John does homage to Philip for his continental lands

1191
Richard defeats Saladin's army in the Battle of Arsuf

1192
Richard is taken hostage on his way home from the crusade

1199
Richard dies after being wounded in France

1200
John marries Isabelle of Angouleme in France

1194
Richard is released from captivity

1202
Philip declares that John's lands in France are forfeit

1194–99 Richard begins five years of warfare against Philip II

1202
John defeats and captures Arthur in the Battle of Mirebeau

Events abroad

6

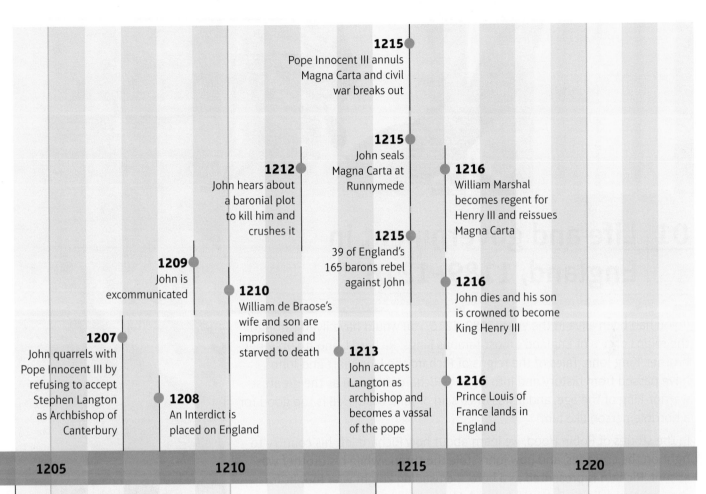

1215
Pope Innocent III annuls Magna Carta and civil war breaks out

1215
John seals Magna Carta at Runnymede

1212
John hears about a baronial plot to kill him and crushes it

1216
William Marshal becomes regent for Henry III and reissues Magna Carta

1209
John is excommunicated

1215
39 of England's 165 barons rebel against John

1210
William de Braose's wife and son are imprisoned and starved to death

1216
John dies and his son is crowned to become King Henry III

1207
John quarrels with Pope Innocent III by refusing to accept Stephen Langton as Archbishop of Canterbury

1213
John accepts Langton as archbishop and becomes a vassal of the pope

1216
Prince Louis of France lands in England

1208
An Interdict is placed on England

1205	1210	1215	1220

1204
Philip II captures Chateau Gaillard

1214
John returns to France with an army

1204
Philip II conquers Normandy

1214
Philip defeats John's allies at the Battle of Bouvines

01 | Life and government in England, 1189–1216

If you had been alive in the years 1189–1216, you would have lived through the reigns of two of England's most famous kings: Richard I, and his younger brother, King John. Tales of the reigns of Richard the Lionheart and John have passed from history and into legend: Richard is known as the greatest warrior-king of the age, and it was once said of John that, 'Hell is too good for a horrible person like him'.

In the stories of Robin Hood, we learn about how Richard left his country to fight on the crusades, and how John stole the throne while his brother was absent. Richard is presented as a hero, a crusading knight who fought for the Christian religion in the Holy Land. Meanwhile, John is condemned as the villain, a man who betrayed his brother and burdened his people with higher and higher taxes. Studying the reigns of these two kings will give you the opportunity to investigate the real Richard and John, and to explore beyond the legends to reach judgements based on historical evidence.

To be successful kings, Richard and John had to be strong military leaders to maintain peace in their lands, to enforce the law fairly and build strong relationships with their more powerful subjects and the Church. It was not easy for a king to achieve all of these aims: for example, it was very difficult to balance the need to spend enough money to win wars, without taxing subjects so much that they became rebellious. However, a king had to meet the expectations of their subjects as any sign of weakness could lead to a civil war.

Learning outcomes

In this chapter you will find out:

- how the feudal system worked
- how medieval kingship worked and the ways in which Richard I and King John secured the throne
- how England was governed under Richard I and King John
- how English society was organised.

1.1 The feudal system

1.1 The feudal system

Learning outcomes

- Understand the nature of the feudal system in this period.
- Understand the role and influence of the Church in England.

England in 1189 was a strange and foreign land compared to the England of today. Our attitude towards equality had no place in the late 12th century. Indeed, these attitudes would have been seen as dangerous because they would challenge the order of society. In 1189, English society was structured into the **feudal system**. This system organised society into a hierarchy based upon the holding of land in return for services.

The feudal hierarchy and the nature of feudalism

The feudal system was introduced into England after William the Conqueror won the Battle of Hastings in 1066. There were four main ranks in the feudal system: the **king**, the **tenants-in-chief**, the **knights** and the **peasants**.

The king

The king was at the top of the feudal hierarchy. He was the most powerful person in the country and all the land belonged to him. He demanded the obedience of the people in his kingdom. In return, the king had a responsibility to protect his people. To do this he needed an army, but this was expensive as soldiers needed paying and providing with horses and weapons. So, the feudal system was used to enable the king to recruit soldiers without paying them.

The tenants-in-chief

The king divided up the land in his kingdom and granted some of it to the tenants-in-chief. They held their land in return for providing services to the king. The most important service was to provide knights for the king's army. They also provided advice to the king and helped to manage the kingdom. Important tenants-in-chief were called **barons**, while others were high-ranking members of the Church, such as archbishops and bishops.

The knights

The knights (or under-tenants) held land from the tenants-in-chief and, in return, they fought on horseback in the king's army when the king demanded knights from his tenants-in-chief. This meant that the knights provided their fighting skills (and paid for their own horses and weapons) in return for their lands. The knights were usually lords of **manorial estates** (see page 30).

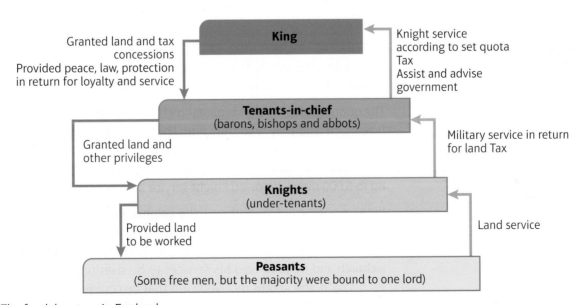

Figure 1.1 The feudal system in England.

The peasants

At the bottom of the feudal system there was a very large class, most of whom were peasants, who held little power. They worked the land for the knights and the tenants-in-chief. In return, the army of knights, recruited by the tenants-in-chief, would protect them from the threat of invasion.

Landholding and homage

The king could not control his lands alone. His land was divided into fiefs. A fief was a portion of land that was granted to a landholder. In return for the land, the landholder had to pledge homage* to his lord* by swearing an **oath of fealty** (or loyalty). When he swore this oath, he became the vassal* of his lord and was required to perform service for him in return for the land that they held. The vassal made his oath in a public ceremony. It was treason to break the oath and the oath-breaker could be punished by death.

The king kept some lands for himself, which became known as the **royal demesne** (or royal lands). The remaining lands were divided up amongst his tenants-in-chief, most of whom were barons. The fiefs that they held were scattered across England. These barons kept some land for their own needs and then sub-divided the rest of their lands to the knights who became their vassals, or under-tenants. The knights also divided out their land among the peasants who lived on it. The peasants held strips of land and farmed it in return for the protection provided to them by the knights.

Knight service

Knight service was the duty that knights owed to their lord in return for holding their land. The tenants-in-chief granted lands, known as a knight's fee, to knights and in return the knights performed certain duties.

- To serve in the king's army for at least two months at his own expense. This included providing his own horse, weapons and armour. If a conflict lasted for longer, then he had to be kept on at the king's expense.
- To perform up to 40 days' service in guarding the lord's castle and in training.
- To help raise money to pay the ransom* of his lord if he was captured in battle and imprisoned.

The quota of knights that tenants-in-chief owed to the king depended on how much land they held from him. The quota was known as the *servitium debitum* and the number of knights owed by the tenants-in-chief ranged from a handful to some 50 or 60 knights. Across the whole of England, there were up to 5,000 men who owed knight service in return for their land.

In the ceremony of knighthood, the knights were presented with a sword and belt and struck gently on the back of the neck with their sword. This was known as dubbing. The new knight also placed his sword on the altar in a church and he promised his services to his overlord and to God. In return for his oath, the knight received land that he could rent out to those below him in the feudal system. The rents provided knights with enough money to support themselves and their family, but they were not necessarily rich.

Key terms

Homage*

The public demonstration of loyalty where a vassal swore an oath of fealty to his lord.

Lord*

A general term used to describe the person (either a tenant-in-chief or a knight) who granted land to a vassal and received homage in return. A lord might also be called a vassal's overlord.

Vassal*

A man who held land (known as a fief) under the feudal system and had done homage to his lord for that land.

Key term

Ransom*

A payment demanded for the release of a prisoner. During wars, knights, barons and even kings were often captured, instead of killed, so that large ransoms could be demanded.

Source A

A 12th-century wall painting from a chapel in France (Cressac-Saint-Genis). It shows a knight in his armour, with a lance and shield, and mounted on horseback.

Extend your knowledge

Household knights

There was also another group of knights: household knights. They did not hold land from their lord, instead they were maintained by the lord as a member of his household and he provided all their food and accommodation. The king had to keep a careful watch on the number of household knights that a baron kept. If it was very large, it might mean that the baron was keeping a private army. This could be a threat to the king if the baron decided to rebel.

Labour service

The lowest ranks of society came below the knights. These included: freemen*, villeins* (or serfs) and cottars*. Collectively, these people are usually referred to as peasants, and the majority of peasants were villeins. The peasants produced all of the food for the country's population to eat. In return for their land, villeins and cottars had a feudal duty to perform labour service for the knights and the tenants-in-chief.

- The villeins had to work for the lord on his land on certain days of the week. This work was known as 'week-work'.
- In addition, the villeins had to work for the lord gathering in the harvest. This work was known as 'boon-work'.
- The cottars worked for one day a week on their lord's land.
- Freemen did not have to work on the lord's land, they paid a rent instead.

Peasants did not owe military service. It was the duty of their overlord to protect them.

Forfeiture

Forfeiture helped the feudal system to function properly. If a vassal did not perform his service as he had sworn to do on oath, their lord could take their land away. This was known as **forfeiture**. For example, if a knight did not turn up to fight when he was summoned to perform his knight service, his land was forfeit to their lord. The lord could then grant that land to a faithful vassal.

Key terms

Freeman*
A peasant who paid rent for their land. They were free to move as they liked.

Villein*
A peasant who was the property of their lord. A villein, unlike a freeman, could not move to another village in search of a better life.

Cottar*
A peasant who held a cottage with a small piece of land attached in return for labour services.

Source B

An example of forfeiture taken from the local court records in the reign of King John. The source is referring to the period 1200–14 when John was fighting against the French king, Philip II.

... the manor of Chinnole along with the hamlet of Sydenham was held... [by Walter de Vernon] from the lord king of England... as one knight's fee. [B]ecause Walter de Vernon refused to perform his due service from the manor to King John (in the time of the war which sprang up between the king and the king of France), [the king]... seized that manor together with its [lands] and removed Walter de Vernon... from the possession of the manor forever.

Activities   ?

1. Look at Source B. Identify the reason why Walter de Vernon forfeited his lands to John.

2. Using your knowledge of forfeiture, work with a partner to expand on the reason you have identified and write a short paragraph to explain why Walter de Vernon forfeited his lands.

3. Draw a flow diagram showing the relationship between different feudal vassals and their overlords. Include the duties and services that they owed to one another on the diagram.

Exam-style question, Section B

Describe **two** features of landholding in the years 1189–1216.   **4 marks**

Exam tip

This question is asking you to select and communicate information. You need to begin by identifying two features. Then, you need to give details to support each of the features you have identified. Don't spend too long on this kind of question as it's only worth 4 marks.

Role and influence of the Church

In the medieval world, religion was at the centre of most people's lives. The purpose of life was to earn a place in heaven, and every major stage of life was influenced by religion. People were expected to attend religious services frequently, and to celebrate the many feast days in the Church calendar. People had to participate in these services and feasts if they were to go to heaven when they died.

The majority of people in Western Europe were Catholic Christians and the Catholic Church was controlled by the pope, who was based in Rome. The pope was regarded as God's representative on Earth, which meant that all Catholics, even kings, were subject to his authority. Kings did have some control over the Church in their own country and they expected to have a say in the appointment of key Church officials, especially archbishops and bishops. However, this issue sometimes led to conflict with the pope.

The Church was very wealthy. Many people donated money or land to the Church, often in their wills. They did this so that members of the Church would pray for them after they died, which would help them get to heaven. The Church earned rents from its land and profits from the agricultural work done on it. By the 13th century, wool earned the Church a lot of money.

The structure of the Church

The most important churchman (or cleric) in England was the Archbishop of Canterbury. He supervised all of England's clergy. He was supported by the Archbishop of York, who supervised the Church in the north of England, and by the other bishops ranked below him. The bishops managed an area called a diocese. They were responsible for the priests and monks in their diocese.

The Church in the feudal system

The clergy's main role was to care for the spiritual welfare of the people by making sure that they correctly followed the teachings of the Church, but they were also an important part of the feudal system. The archbishops and bishops held land as vassals of the king, and the Church owned about 20% of the land in England. This land could not be taken away from the Church, but churchmen were expected to perform duties for it. Their first duty was to perform church services. They carried out baptisms, marriages and burials as well as daily services. In addition, important churchmen, such as the archbishops, bishops and abbots, had to supply a quota of knights for the king's army.

Many churchmen were educated and could read and write. This meant that they often became **clerks** (record-keepers, also known as clerics) in baronial and royal households. Some important churchmen became leading members of the government: for example, the king's chancellor* was always a cleric. In this way, the Church had an influence on the king's decisions. The king relied upon clerics for the day-to-day government of the kingdom, so it was important for him to remain on good terms with the Church.

Key term

Chancellor*

The head of the chancery, the government body which was responsible for producing official documents. The chancellor was the keeper of the Great Seal, which was used to show that the king had approved certain documents.

Ensure people correctly follow Church teachings

Perform daily church services, as well as things like baptisms, marriages and funerals

Supply a quota of knights for the king's army (only important churchmen)

Act as clerks in baronial or royal households

Advise the king (only important churchmen)

Figure 1.2 The various duties of clerics.

The king expected his clergy to be loyal to him. This could be a problem if he came into conflict with the pope as the clergy regarded the pope as their supreme overlord. This made the relationship between the king and the Church very complicated.

- The king wanted the clergy to recognise his authority and to obey his laws. He expected to be able to use feudal punishments, like forfeiture, against clerics who broke his laws.

- The pope could use his weapons of Interdict* and excommunication* if he believed a serious offence against the Church had been committed. It made life very difficult if the king, or a leading baron, was excommunicated as Christians were forbidden to associate with a person who had been excommunicated.

Key terms

Interdict*

The withdrawal of church services from an individual or country. If a country was placed under an Interdict then there could be no church services, baptisms, weddings or funerals. Without these services, people believed it was impossible to go to heaven.

Excommunication*

The exclusion of an individual from the Church and all its services. It was the most serious punishment used by the Church: a person who was excommunicated would go to hell. However, it was possible for the pope to lift the sentence of excommunication if the individual reformed their behaviour.

Summary

- English society was organised into a hierarchical system called feudalism.
- Tenants-in-chief had to supply a quota of knights to the king as part of their feudal duty.
- Knight service required knights to fight in the king's army for two months and to do 40 days' service in their lord's castle.
- Peasants had to do labour service on their lord's land as part of their feudal duty.
- Vassals who failed to do their feudal duty forfeited their lands.
- The Church was a powerful institution that looked after the spiritual welfare of the people. Leading churchmen advised the king in the government.

Checkpoint

Strengthen

S1 What is a fief?

S2 What is the difference between a tenant-in-chief (e.g. a baron) and a knight?

S3 Give two examples of the influence of the Church in England at this time.

Challenge

C1 What consequences did a vassal face if they broke their oath of fealty?

C2 Explain why a king would want to maintain good relations with the Church in this period.

How confident do you feel about your answers to these questions? If you are not sure you answered them well, form a group with other students, discuss the answers and then record your conclusions.

1.2 Kingship and succession

Learning outcomes

- Understand the nature of kingship in this period.
- Understand how Richard became king and his character.
- Understand how John became king and his character.

The nature of kingship

A medieval monarch was a powerful ruler with complete responsibility for governing his kingdom. This meant that the character and abilities of the king were of great importance. The king needed to be a strong ruler to control his kingdom, to enforce justice and to keep the kingdom safe from attack. The whole nation depended upon him to do this effectively.

Source A

Richard I illustrated in the 13th-century chronicle the *Historia Anglorum, Chronica* by Matthew Paris. Richard is shown with the symbols of his power, including the crown on his head and the sword in his hand. He holds a church in one hand to show his close relationship with the Church.

Rights of succession*

In the 11th century the Normans introduced the principle of **primogeniture**. According to this principle, the eldest son inherits his father's title and all his lands. In the case of a king, it meant that the eldest legitimate son would inherit the throne (a child was legitimate if they were born to the queen while she was married to the king). However, by the late 12th century, this principle had not been fully established for the succession of kings. In fact, Richard I was the first English king for more than 100 years to inherit the throne from his father. In that time, kings had been nominated by the previous king, or had been chosen by the leading barons in the kingdom. The succession was important because if it was unclear who would be the next monarch then there could be a civil war.

Key term

Succession*

The sequence by which one person follows another to inherit a throne, title or lands.

Rights of kingship

From the moment a king was anointed with holy oils at his coronation (the ceremony where a monarch is crowned), he took the title of *rex*, or king, and was given divine authority. This meant that he was chosen by God to be king and his subjects could not question his authority. It was not until the reign of King John and the issuing of Magna Carta that subjects attempted to place some controls on the king (see pages 80–84).

Duties

The king was the greatest authority in the kingdom. He was the chief decision-maker, and both foreign and domestic policy were decided by him. However, a king could not do exactly as he pleased. During the coronation the king had to make an oath where he promised to perform certain duties. In the oath, the king promised to keep the peace. He also promised to protect his people by punishing excessive greed of feudal lords, and to maintain justice.

The king was the supreme law maker, and he had a duty to show fairness and mercy in his judgements. In order to fulfil his oath, the king, or his agents, needed to travel around the country, hearing cases and making judgements. This itinerant kingship* helped the king to build relationships with his most important nobles by meeting with them and staying in their castles.

> ### Key term
>
> **Itinerant kingship***
>
> The practice of the king and his court travelling from place to place around the country.

One of the king's most important duties was to protect his kingdom and its people from foreign attack and civil wars. Therefore, a king needed to have effective military skills. He needed to be able to plan campaigns, direct his armies and to choose capable military leaders. The king often led the army himself as a warrior. Richard I is one of the greatest examples of a warrior-king.

Rituals and display

A medieval king needed to be seen by his subjects to reinforce his authority. Formal occasions and rituals were arranged to enable the king to do this. The greatest ritual was the coronation, where the king was anointed with holy oils and crowned in front of the most important nobles and clerics. However, more regular displays of the king's majesty were also needed. The system of itinerant kingship helped with this. The king was seen by his subjects when he held his courts across the country.

Since the reign of William the Conqueror, kings had taken part in a ritual of '**crown-wearings**'. When he was present in England, the king wore his crown in three different places at three important times in the year: in Winchester (at Easter), in Gloucester (at Christmas) and in Westminster (at Witsun – the seventh Sunday after Easter). The crown-wearings were important occasions and were accompanied by pageants and feasts. Rituals and public displays of kingship, like crown-wearings, encouraged loyalty to the monarch as they reminded people of his power and authority.

Richard I as king

Richard I, known as *Coeur de Lion* (or Lionheart), is perhaps the most famous English medieval king. He was the third son of Henry II and Eleanor of Aquitaine. Richard developed a reputation as an outstanding warrior and king while he was alive, and this reputation has been enhanced in myth and legend ever since.

Figure 1.3 The statue of Richard the Lionheart, outside the Houses of Parliament. The statue was erected in 1860. It is evidence of how Richard has been seen as a great warrior-king and how his popularity has lasted into modern times.

Richard's claim to the throne

In 1189, when Henry II died, Richard was his eldest surviving legitimate son. While the principle of primogeniture, as mentioned earlier, had not yet been established as the sole reason for the succession of a king, Richard had an excellent claim to the throne. Richard was the favourite son of his mother, Eleanor, and he had been made Duke of Aquitaine in 1172. Aquitaine was a vast territory in southern France and brought Richard both wealth and power. By contrast, his younger brother, John, who was the favourite of his father, possessed no lands at all at the time of Henry's death.

Although Richard had a good claim to the throne, he feared that Henry intended to make John the king of England after his death. This fear led him to fight alongside the French king, Philip II, against his father in 1187–89 and capture land in the Angevin Empire*.

Key term

Angevin Empire*

The lands that Henry II and his family held in England, Wales and France. The empire stretched from Northumbria in England to the Pyrenees on the border with Spain. The name Angevin comes from Anjou, the county Henry inherited from his father.

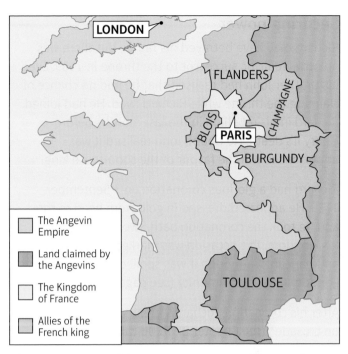

Figure 1.5 A map of the Angevin Empire at the time of Richard's succession in 1189. Note that the Angevin Empire is much larger than the Kingdom of France.

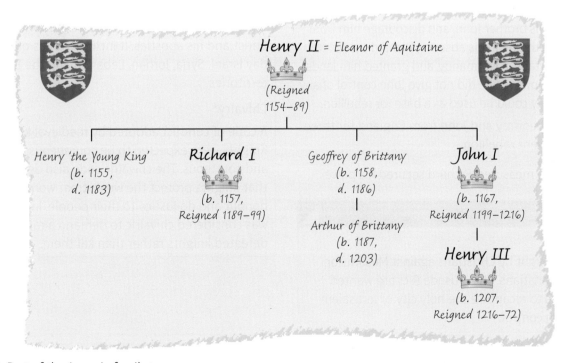

Figure 1.4 Part of the Angevin family tree.

Securing power

Richard may have betrayed his father, but there was no other realistic successor to the throne in 1189. Even his brother John had realised that he had no chance of claiming the throne while Richard lived. He had joined Richard in his rebellion in the last months before Henry II's death. No doubt, John realised it was important to win the favour of the soon-to-be king.

Richard had a glorious coronation on 3 September 1189. He appeared dressed in gold from head to toe and he took the coronation oath, swearing to protect his kingdom. The occasion was marked by feasting and pageants, although it was spoiled by an attack on London's Jewish community (see page 35).

After his coronation, Richard's greatest desire was to go on crusade* (see Chapter 2). To do this, he needed to secure his kingdom.

- He made peace with the men who had fought with his father against him.
- He appointed William Longchamp as his chancellor to manage the kingdom in his absence.
- He appointed his half-brother Geoffrey (one of Henry II's illegitimate children) as Archbishop of York. Richard feared that Geoffrey might seize the throne, so he made him an archbishop because a cleric could not become king.
- To appease his brother John, and discourage him from claiming the throne in his absence, Richard made him Count of Mortain, in Normandy, and granted him lands in England. However, he did not give John control of any castles as they could be used as a base for rebellion.
- He banned Geoffrey and John from England for three years to prevent rebellion.

By taking these measures, Richard secured his power.

Key term

Crusade*

A holy war fought by Christians against Muslims or other non-Christians. The crusade Richard wanted to go on was to recapture the holy city of Jerusalem from Muslim control.

Richard's character

Richard is often regarded as the model of a medieval king. At the time, he was seen as a great warrior who did his Christian duty by leading a crusade to the Holy Land*. His personality, his success in battle and his charisma helped him to gain the loyalty of his subjects.

Richard's character was formed in Aquitaine where he spent much of his teenage years. As a young man, Richard was deeply influenced by the code of chivalry* which guided his training as a knight and his behaviour in battle. On the other hand, in spite of his love of chivalry, he also had a practical view of warfare. He believed that problems could be solved by battle and he admired ruthlessness. Richard also had less attractive qualities: his time in Aquitaine made him arrogant and selfish, and on three occasions he had broken his feudal oath and rebelled against his father.

Away from the battlefield, chivalry continued to play an important part in his behaviour. He developed chivalric ideas of courtly love, which is an idealised form of love where men almost worship women in poetry and song. Richard's enthusiasm for courtly love influenced the poetry and music that he wrote.

Key terms

The Holy Land*

The area of the Middle East associated with Jesus Christ and his apostles. It includes areas of modern day Israel, Syria, Jordan, Lebanon and the Palestinian territories.

Chivalry*

A code of conduct adopted by medieval knights. Knights were expected to be courageous, honourable and courteous. The chivalric code also demanded that knights protect the weak, treat women with honour and do justice to their people. In battle, it was considered chivalric to demand a ransom for defeated knights rather than kill them.

Interpretation 1

Historian Frank Barlow gives his opinion of Richard's character in his book *The Feudal Kingdom of England 1042–1216* (1999).

Richard Coeur-de-Lion was a great man, perhaps too great a man… Richard was at his finest superhuman, at his worst unpleasant and inhumane. Although pre-eminent [outstanding] as a soldier and engineer, he was shrewd in politics and also capable of diplomacy on the grand scale. More generous than his father, nobler, more imaginative, less careful, he bid for more glittering prizes and took far graver risks. Not as clever as Philip [the king of France], more wayward, he tried by tremendous efforts to win back those advantages which in his rasher moments he gave his rival. During his short life his reputation was fabulous…

Activities ?

1 Working with a partner, list three reasons why Richard I became king.

2 Write a paragraph that explains how Richard secured his power as king.

3 Read Interpretation 1. Working in a small group, find examples in the chapter that support Barlow's opinions about Richard, and write your own summary of Richard's character.

Exam-style question, Section B

Explain why Richard became king in 1189.

You may use the following in your answer:

• Richard's claim to the throne

• Richard's character.

You **must** also use information of your own. **12 marks**

Exam tip

This question is about causation. A good answer should give at least three reasons and clearly explain how they led to the outcome. So, you would need to identify at least one more reason and explain why they led to Richard's succession to the throne.

John as king

If Richard I is often regarded as the greatest medieval king, then John is usually portrayed as the worst. This image of a villainous king has been preserved in the tales of Robin Hood and it is not entirely wrong. John did seize control of England during Richard's absence on crusade and he imposed heavy taxes during his reign. However, John's image has developed through myth and legend.

Source B

King John illustrated in the 13th-century chronicle the *Historia Anglorum, Chronica* by Matthew Paris. John is posed in a very similar way to the portrait of Richard in Source A on page 15, but John is not holding a sword. This could be a criticism of John's skills as a warrior.

John's claim to the throne

John was the fifth and last son of Henry and Eleanor. By the time he reached his teenage years, his parents' land was already divided between his older brothers and so John became known as 'Lackland'. Henry's plan for John to become Lord of Ireland fell through when, on expedition in 1185, John insulted the Irish princes by pulling their beards. John was his father's favourite and was, it seems, being trained for kingship by him. However, John was no match for Richard as a soldier and because of this there was little chance he could become king while Richard was alive.

Richard's succession had been very straightforward. He was the oldest legitimate son of his father and the popular choice of the Angevin barons. John's claim was much more complicated. He had the following factors in his favour.

- His claim, in 1199, was supported by Eleanor of Aquitaine, William Marshal (one of the greatest knights of his era and an important baron) and Hubert Walter, the Archbishop of Canterbury.
- He was the preferred candidate for the English and Norman barons.
- He was, at 31 years old, in the prime of his life and had proven himself as a warrior by fighting against the French king with Richard in 1194–99. He had demonstrated that he possessed some of the experience and qualities that were required in a king.

However, he was not the only claimant to the throne.

- His elder brother Geoffrey, Duke of Brittany (who had died in 1186), had a son, Arthur. On the principle of primogeniture, Arthur had a better claim to the throne than John.
- The barons in Brittany, and some in Anjou, preferred Arthur's claim.
- Arthur's claim was supported by the king of France.

Securing power

Fortunately for John, his claim to the throne of England was accepted after Richard's death. Arthur was only 12 at the time and was regarded as a foreigner by the English. With the support of Eleanor, the English barons were encouraged to accept John. He was crowned king on 27 May 1199 and took the oath to protect the Church, abolish bad laws and do justice to his people. John then showed his religious devotion by visiting the shrines at Canterbury and at Bury St Edmunds. Demonstrating good judgement, John appointed a loyal baron to protect the north of his kingdom from the threat of Scotland.

Just four weeks later, John left for France to secure the continental lands of the Angevin Empire. He left the government of England in the hands of trusted men who had served Richard loyally. In May 1200, John met with the French king, Philip II, and they agreed a peace treaty.

- John agreed to give some Angevin lands to Philip.
- John agreed to do homage to Philip for his continental lands and pay £13,500, which was the feudal fine John had to pay his overlord for his inheritance of the lands. (The French king was overlord of the lands in France and, in theory, the king of England was his vassal.)
- Philip dropped his support for Arthur's claim to the throne.

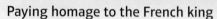

Extend your knowledge

Paying homage to the French king

Henry II had made his sons do homage to the French king for their lands in France. However, he had always been careful not to do homage himself. The Angevin lands were larger than the territory of the French king. This meant that the French king found it almost impossible to force the English king to behave as a vassal. Richard followed his father's lead and would not do homage as king. Many historians believe that John made a mistake in doing homage to Philip. Later, it would give Philip the right to declare that John was a disobedient vassal and that his lands were forfeit.

The murder of Prince Arthur

The peace did not last long. By 1200, Philip II and John were back at war with one another and, once again, Arthur joined Philip. John was furious. He had made Arthur do homage to him for Brittany, and Arthur had broken his feudal oath by siding with Philip. In August 1202, Arthur was captured after a battle at Mirebeau. The events that followed severely damaged John's reputation. Arthur was kept imprisoned in chains while John decided what to do with him.

- According to the chivalric code, John should have ransomed him.
- Alternatively, he could have tried him as a traitor.

However, John did neither. Contemporary accounts tell us that John ordered that Arthur should be castrated and blinded. However, Arthur's gaolers refused to do this. Sometime after this, either John, or someone close to him, stabbed Arthur to death and dumped his body in the River Seine, weighted down by a stone. Even John's supporters were horrified by his treatment of his nephew, and many trusted Norman barons began to change sides to support Philip II.

Source C

An account of Arthur's death in the chronicle of 1202 written by the monks at the abbey of Margam in Glamorgan, Wales.

... after dinner on the Thursday before Easter when, he [King John] was drunk and possessed by the devil, he slew him [Arthur] with his own hand, and tying a heavy stone to the body cast it into the Seine. It was discovered by a fisherman in his net, and... was taken for secret burial in fear of the tyrant [John]...

Interpretation 2

Ralph V. Turner gives his view on the murder of Arthur in *King John: England's Evil King?* (2005).

In the Middle Ages, even the most brutal baron had a strong family feeling that made him incapable of condoning parricide [approving the murder of a relative]. Yet young Arthur was a traitor to his sworn lord, captured while fighting against him, who could lawfully have been condemned to death; and Pope Innocent III was not much upset when he learned later that John had killed him. Nonetheless, the boy's murder was an error in political judgement as well as a criminal act, offsetting everything that John had won at Mirebeau.

John's character

In 1199, John was regarded by the English barons as the best candidate for the throne, and John had learnt from his father many of the qualities needed to be a good king. John had also spent some of his youth in England and he developed an understanding of its system of government. His time in England meant that he was regarded as English and at first this helped to encourage loyalty from his barons.

John's reign began well when he selected capable men to manage England while he was absent in France. This shows intelligence and good judgement. John had also proven himself to be a capable military leader while supporting Richard's wars against the French. This experience was highly valued in an era when the king played a key role in warfare. However, there were flaws in his character and behaviour that were revealed early on in his reign. His short temper, cruelty and rash behaviour was demonstrated in his decision to murder Prince Arthur. John also did not trust many people and his suspicious nature meant that his subjects had little loyalty to him.

Activities

1 Imagine that everyone in your class is one of John's barons. It is your task to decide what should happen to Prince Arthur after his capture. Here are the possible choices:
   a Put Arthur on trial for treason.
   b Ransom Arthur to the Bretons or to Philip.
   c Offer Arthur rewards in lands, titles and money to switch sides.
   d Murder Arthur.
   With a fellow baron, discuss and write down the pros and cons of each of the choices.
2 Join with another pair of barons and, in your group, pick the action that you all agree would be best. Write a short paragraph to explain your decision.
3 One person will need to take the role of King John. Each group of four barons must present their choice to John and persuade him to agree to it.

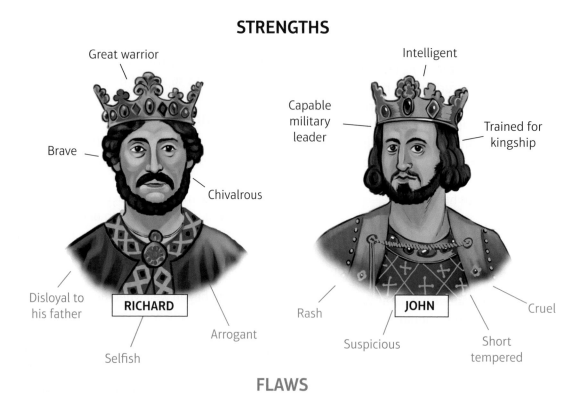

STRENGTHS

FLAWS

Figure 1.6 Richard and John's strengths and flaws.

Summary

- A medieval king was responsible for protecting his people, ensuring justice and for making war. He was seen as being chosen by God and his authority could not be questioned.
- Richard I succeeded to the throne as his father's eldest surviving legitimate son. He made peace with the French king and granted land to John to discourage him from rebellion.
- Richard is often regarded as the ideal medieval king.
- King John secured the throne against the claims of his nephew, Arthur. He was supported by his mother, Eleanor, and many of the leading barons in the Angevin Empire.
- John is often regarded as the worst medieval king.

Checkpoint

Strengthen

S1 Outline the aspects of Richard I's character that make him appear to be the ideal medieval king.

S2 Make a list of the positive qualities in John's character that suggested he could be a good king.

S3 Briefly explain what happened to John's nephew, Arthur.

Challenge

C1 Explain the measures that Richard put into place to keep his kingdom safe while he was on crusade.

C2 In your own words, explain how John became king.

How confident do you feel about your answers to these questions? If you are not sure you answered them well, re-read the section on medieval kingship and write a summary of the key points.

1.3 Royal government and finances

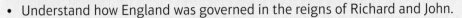

Learning outcomes

- Understand how England was governed in the reigns of Richard and John.
- Understand how royal revenue was raised and the role of sheriffs.

Royal government in the Middle Ages was focused on maintaining law and order, and providing taxes to help the king defend his kingdom. A medieval king was expected to only call upon his subjects for taxation in times of extraordinary need. Both Richard and John demanded vast sums of money from their subjects.

- Richard needed money to fund his crusade.
- Richard needed money to be ransomed from captivity in 1194 (see pages 56–58).
- Both Richard and John needed huge sums to pay for their wars against France.

The payment of taxes was never popular. The heavy demands made by John, in particular, is one reason why he was regarded as a bad king.

The sums of money that the king could collect from his lands and through taxes might seem small by modern standards, but at that time, the English kings were amongst the wealthiest monarchs in Europe. Between 1194 and 1198, Richard had an annual income of about £25,000. John's income was usually between £22,000 and £25,000, but sometimes he was able to gather in huge incomes; the accounts for 1211 suggested that he collected in £83,291.

How England was governed in Richard's absence, 1189–99

Richard was only present in England for six months during his ten year reign. In 1189, he came to England to be crowned and to raise money for his crusade.

- Richard sold lands and titles to the highest bidders. He even said he would sell London if he could find a buyer.
- He managed to raise over £31,000 to fund his crusade.

Richard also had to consider how England would be governed in his absence. It was not unusual for the king to be absent from his kingdom. The important thing was to make sure that the kingdom would be well governed and

at peace while he was away. First, Richard needed to make sure it was protected from the claims of his rivals.

- An agreement was made with the Scottish king, William the Lion, where he was freed from his obligation to do homage to Richard. In return, William abandoned his claim to lands in the north of England.
- He provided his brother John and half-brother Geoffrey with lands and titles, and banned them from England for three years (see page 18).

Richard then needed to appoint trustworthy officials who could manage the government in his absence. Richard chose a loyal, royal servant, William Longchamp, to be his chancellor. As chancellor, it was Longchamp's duty to manage the government by the use of charters* and writs*, which outlined the decisions of the king and enabled the chancellor to rule on the king's behalf when he was absent. Longchamp was also made a justiciar*. Justiciars were responsible for justice and they travelled from shire to shire hearing cases in the courts and giving royal judgement.

After three months, Richard had settled the government of his kingdom and he departed on crusade.

Key terms

Charter*

A document that outlines rights, especially property rights. Royal charters carried the royal seal which meant the rights would be enforced with royal authority.

Writ*

A document that granted authority or issued a command.

Justiciar*

An officer of the king's court who heard law cases and made judgements on the king's behalf. He had the authority of a king during the king's absence from the kingdom.

1.3 Royal government and finances

Regent*

A person who is appointed to rule a kingdom because the king is either absent, a minor or incapable of ruling.

Prince John's rebellion

By 1191, John was allowed into England and it was not long before the peaceful government that Richard established broke down. John set up his own court and he was soon collecting taxes on his own behalf. Then, John seized control of Nottingham and Tickhill castles. He was helped in his rebellion by a number of barons who despised William Longchamp. The English barons hated him because he had paid £3,000 to be appointed chancellor and because he was arrogant in his treatment of them. In October 1191, at a meeting in London, the barons decided that John should be regent* while Richard was absent. Longchamp was deposed and John replaced him as chancellor with Walter of Coutances.

Source A

The Great Seal of Richard the Lionheart. The seal was attached to documents to give them royal authority. Use of this seal gave royal authority to those who ruled England in Richard's absence.

Extend your knowledge

William Longchamp

If Richard had possessed better knowledge of England, he may not have left it in Longchamp's hands. Longchamp was unacceptable to the English barons, not just because he was a Norman with little knowledge of English government, but also because of his arrogance towards the English barons. One of his actions that greatly angered the barons was to replace many sheriffs with his own men (see page 29 for more on sheriffs). This caused anger because many of the men that were replaced had paid Richard to appoint them as sheriffs.

The government of England, 1194–99

Richard's return to England from crusade was delayed by his capture and imprisonment in 1192–94. During this period, John ruled as regent. John's actions made him very unpopular.

- Heavy taxes were imposed to pay Richard's ransom, and also to pay for John's campaigns in France.
- John announced that Richard was dead and that he was the legitimate king, only to be caught out when a letter arrived announcing that Richard was alive and being held prisoner in Germany.
- John allied with Philip II to seize Richard's lands in France.

In February 1194, Richard was released and John had to throw himself on the mercy of his brother. Richard forgave him, but he humiliated John (who was 27 years old) by saying: 'Have no fear, John, you are but a child. It is those who led you astray who will be punished'.

Richard appointed Hubert Walter, the Archbishop of Canterbury, as justiciar. After three months, Richard departed for the continent and did not return to England again. Walter established an effective system of justice by selecting four knights in every hundred* to take charge of the system of justice in their area. England was governed peacefully until Richard's death in 1199.

Key term

Hundred*

A subdivision of a shire. The whole of England was divided up into areas of land called shires for administrative purposes and each shire was then divided into smaller units called hundreds.

How England was governed under King John, 1199–1216

In the first six years of John's reign, his main focus was on defending his lands in France. This meant there was no significant change in the system of government in England because the country had been governed without the king's presence for most of Richard's reign. Geoffrey Fitz Peter, who had been one of Richard's justiciars, acted as regent for John. However, in 1204, John lost control of Normandy and returned to England. After that, John's continued presence in England created problems.

There were several reasons why John's rule became increasingly unpopular.

- John chose '**new men**' rather than barons to advise him, which angered the barons as they expected to be called upon to advise the king. John's 'new men' were totally dependent on him for their wealth, and exploited their position to gain large rewards for their advice. In the meantime, the feudal barons were increasingly excluded from government.

- John virtually closed down the Court of the King's Bench* at Westminster and ended the practice of sending his royal justices out to hear cases in the shires. Cases could only be heard in the royal court when John was present. This meant that John himself was blamed by barons when judgements went against them.

- John was cruel in his punishment of those who displeased him. For example, one of his leading barons, William de Braose, owed a large debt to John. He was forced to flee the country, but his wife and eldest son were captured and starved to death in prison. Incidents like this made the barons hate and fear John.

There's more on the unpopularity of John's kingship in Chapter 3.

John was interested in the way government worked and in record-keeping. This is shown by the huge increase in the government records kept in his reign. However, medieval government relied on the king working together with his barons to control the kingdom, but John failed to do this because he did not trust them.

Source B

Peter des Roches' tomb in Winchester Cathedral, Hampshire. He was one of John's 'new men' and his loyalty to John led to him being made bishop of Winchester. His importance is indicated by his splendid tomb.

Activities

1 Richard did a lot of things to try to make his kingdom safe in his absence. Which was the most important and why?

2 Write a paragraph to explain why Richard's measures to protect his kingdom failed.

3 Working with a partner, make lists of the positive and negative aspects of Richard's government. Then, write a judgement on whether you think Richard was an effective king.

Key term

The Court of the King's Bench*
The royal law court at Westminster, which served as a headquarters for the royal justices. The royal justices recorded the judgements they made in the cases that they heard around the country. These records helped them to make judgements on similar cases in future.

Interpretation 1

David Starkey comments on John's style of ruling in *Crown and Country: A History of England Through Monarchy* (2010).

John's obsession for record-keeping was a sign not of strength, but of weakness. He was so keen on documentation because he was so mistrustful of his subjects, and his subjects in turn distrusted a king who was always nit-picking and always eager to revive an old, outdated royal imposition or invent a new one. The result was tax, tax and more tax.

Key term

Debasement*
The practice of lowering the value of the currency. In the 13th century, some individuals clipped the silver from coins, so that they weighed less, and melted down the clippings to produce more silver coins to exchange for goods. Debasement was a major problem in John's reign and it resulted in sellers demanding more coins for their goods, pushing up prices.

Royal revenues

Both Richard and John made huge demands on their subjects for money. The crusades and war in France, as well as the cost of Richard's ransom, meant that they had to call upon their subjects for taxes. In addition, prices were rising rapidly in the early 13th century because a large number of silver pennies were imported into England from the continent and because of the debasement* of the coinage. This meant the value of revenues from royal lands fell.

Source C

Officers receiving and weighing coins at the exchequer (the royal counting house) in the 12th century. Coins were brought to the exchequer and weighed to ensure that they were the correct weight.

Extend your knowledge

John's cruel methods
John was also unpopular because of the cruel methods he used in collecting the taxes. In 1210, a Jew from Bristol refused to pay his tallage. John ordered that he should lose a tooth for every day he refused to pay. On the seventh day he paid his tax.

The royal demesne

The land that was held directly by the king was known as the royal demesne. This land provided the king with the money from rent to pay his expenses in times of peace. The royal demesne was made up of royal hunting forests, royal manor estates (with their attached villages) and towns. The ownership of towns was very profitable for the king. He could charge rents to those living in the towns and collect taxes from those who sold goods in them.

Tallage

Tallage was a compulsory land tax that was paid by the tenants of the royal demesne, including those living in royal towns. These tenants included townsmen and peasants. Some historians claim that the payment of tallage was the mark of 'inferior status' because it was only paid by the lower classes, and not by the barons and knights. It was unpopular for this reason, but also because it could be demanded by the king, or a lord, and no appeal against it was allowed. There was no fixed sum and so the amounts demanded were often seen as unreasonably high.

Feudal incidents

Medieval kings were allowed to call upon their vassals to make certain payments. These payments are known as feudal incidents and they are summarised in Figure 1.7.

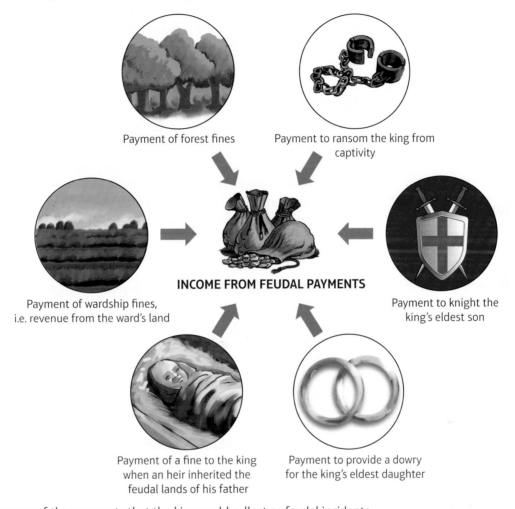

Figure 1.7 A summary of the payments that the king could collect as feudal incidents.

Wardship fines

One of the most profitable feudal incidents was the wardship fine. If a baron died while his heir was under age (a minor), his land returned to the king, and the heir, along with his siblings, became wards of the king. The king was responsible for the wards until the baron's heir became an adult. The king decided where the wards would live, as well as the education and training they received. This is known as wardship. In return, the king kept the revenues from the baron's land until the heir reached adulthood. The lands would then be returned to the heir on payment of a fine, known as a wardship fine. Under John, the amount charged for wardship fines increased by 300% compared to the fine charged by

Henry II. The king could also claim a fine on the marriage of his ward, and he could organise the marriage of his late vassal's widow, collecting a payment from her new husband. As a result, the king raised a lot of money from wardship.

Forest fines

Areas of land could be designated as 'forest'. This land was under the protection of the king. The king could claim forest fines for those living, working, hunting and foraging on forest land. These fines affected peasants, knights and barons. John increased forest fines in his reign and these fines fell most heavily upon the northern barons.

The profits of justice

Justice was not free and the king could enjoy considerable profits from it. Cases were usually started by the payment of a fee for a writ, which went to the king. John interfered with the progress of cases and this led to some vassals complaining that he sold justice. For example, in 1207 John gave a favourable judgement to the party that offered him three horses in payment for supporting their case.

Scutage

Scutage was a payment made by the holders of a knight's fee in return for not having to fight. Richard and John used this money to pay for engineers, foot soldiers and bowmen in their wars. These soldiers were not included in the feudal army that owed service to the king in return for land, but they were needed both for fighting on an open battlefield and in besieging castles. In addition, campaigns often lasted longer than the 40 days' service owed by knights. Therefore, kings needed to hire professional soldiers, or mercenaries, and they used scutage to pay for them.

King John demanded 11 scutages in 16 years. This greatly angered his barons as it was becoming almost an annual tax, whereas the barons believed it should only be collected in an emergency. Some historians believe that the final scutage demanded in 1214 was one of the main reasons for the rebellion at the end of John's reign (see pages 80–87).

1207 tax on moveables and incomes

In spite of John's demands for taxes and his frequent scutages, he needed more income. At a meeting of his barons, in 1207, he developed a new method of taxation. He demanded the payment of a tax based on the goods and income of every man. He claimed it was needed to pay for a campaign in France. Surprisingly, the tax was approved by the barons present at the meeting.

The tax was set at one shilling in every mark. A mark was worth just over 13 shillings, so the tax became known as a '**Thirteenth**'. The penalties for failure to pay were harsh. Those who tried to avoid paying the tax risked imprisonment and seizure of all their property. It raised £60,000 but was so unpopular that John did not risk collecting it again.

Interpretation 2

Here A.L. Poole argues in his book, *From Domesday Book to Magna Carta 1087–1216* (1993), that John's demands for taxes were not as unreasonable as they seemed to his subjects at the time.

It is unquestionable that the burden of taxation was very largely increased under King John. Scutages had been increased and become almost annual imposts [demands], the lists of amercements [fines] lengthened year by year. John has been severely criticised for his financial extortions [demands], and they met with violent opposition. Yet it should be recognised that prices had risen steeply in the early years of the 13th century; the expenses of government were very heavy. It was not unreasonable to raise a scutage of two or even three marks... when the wages of a knight had more than doubled.

Activity ?

Draw a large concept map for the topic: The King's income. You will need to decide on some categories for your diagram, for example: taxes, feudal incidents, profits from justice, forest fines, tax collection, etc. Use A3 paper and colour-code your categories to help make them more memorable.

The collection of taxes: the role of the sheriffs

The taxes from the royal demesne were collected by an official called a sheriff*. In the time of King Richard, the system of collection was based on a method known as tax farming. The sheriff was set a fixed sum of tax to collect and he could keep any money that he collected in addition to that sum. This meant that sheriffs could become very wealthy, which helps to explain why Richard was able to raise a lot of money for his crusade by selling sheriff offices. The tax farming system continued under John and became increasingly oppressive as sheriffs demanded more and more money. However, John would not allow sheriffs to become rich at his expense. He inspected the records of tax collection and insisted that he got the greatest share of the sums collected.

Key terms

Sheriff*

A royal official who worked for the king to oversee local government issues. He collected taxes, hunted down criminals and often managed a royal castle.

Summary

- Richard I was absent from England for all but six months of his ten year reign. His government was managed by his chancellor or justiciars.
- Prince John seized control of the government in Richard's absence between 1191 and 1194, but it was restored to Richard's justiciar when Richard returned from captivity.
- King John's own government became increasingly unpopular as he was accused of selling justice, treating his subjects cruelly and demanding heavy taxes.
- Richard and John needed high taxes to pay for their wars. In particular, John exploited his feudal rights to raise as much money as he could, which angered the barons.
- The sheriff was the key royal official who collected taxes for the king.

Checkpoint

Strengthen

S1 What was a justiciar?

S2 Give two examples of taxes used by King John.

S3 Look at John's methods of government and raising taxes. Find three examples to illustrate and explain why his methods were so unpopular.

S4 What was the role of the sheriff in the tax system?

Challenge

C1 In your own words, explain the events of John's rebellion in 1191–94.

C2 How does John's government of England compare to Richard's? Think about the following features:
- the personal role of the king,
- their use of royal officials, e.g. justiciars and sheriffs,
- taxation.

How confident do you feel about your answers to these questions? If you are not sure you answered them well, ask your teacher for some hints.

1.4 English society

Learning outcomes

- Understand the nature of country and town life.
- Understand the role and status of Jews in this period.

The vast majority of English people lived and worked on the land in the Middle Ages. Ordinary people faced a constant struggle to provide for their families. Famine and plague were never too far away and life tended to be short. Most people did not live long past 40 years and, for those at the bottom of society, life was often much shorter.

The nature of agriculture and peasant life

The peasantry

The two main types of peasant were villeins and freemen. A villein was the property of the lord and the lord could do as he pleased with him, except kill or injure him. For example, a lord could sell a villein or fine him. Freedom was greatly prized and a lord could give a villein his freedom by issuing a charter. A freeman was free to move as he pleased, he could not be controlled by a lord like a villein.

The medieval manorial estate

Most peasants lived and worked on a manorial estate. These were made up of one or several villages surrounding a manor house in which the lord of the manor or his bailiff* lived. The lord kept some of the land on the estate for himself and the rest was divided up amongst the peasants, for them to farm.

The work on the land was supervised by a reeve*. He divided out the work, and kept the accounts of the sales of produce and the collection of rents. As part of their feudal service, the villeins regularly worked two or three days a week on their lord's land. Freemen, however, only occasionally worked on the lord's land because they paid a rent instead. By the end of the 12th century, the definition of a villein was changing as more villeins were paying rent instead of working for their lord.

Key terms

Bailiff*

An official who took care of a lord's land. Medieval lords held land in different parts of the country so many estates were managed by bailiffs.

Reeve*

An official chosen from the villeins to supervise the farm work. Today we would call a similar person a foreman.

Source A

An image taken from a 13th-century manuscript showing a peasant cutting hay with a scythe.

Farming activities

The type of farming undertaken by the peasants depended on the quality of the land. Most peasants were involved in growing crops. The bulk of these crops provided food to feed their families. The land was usually farmed in the following way.

- The village farming land was divided into two to three large open fields.
- One field was usually left **fallow** (unfarmed) to allow the soil to recover while the others were farmed.

- The fields were divided into strips. Peasants, including the freemen, had strips in different fields so that they would have a share of the best and worst soils.
- The fields were ploughed, sown and harvested by villeins. Cottars often helped at harvest time.
- Every villein had to grow the same crop in the field. The type of crop varied according to the soil type. Barley, wheat, rye and oats were all grown in England in the Middle Ages.
- Villeins would take their crops to the village mill to be ground. They had to pay a fee for using the mill. This was charged by their feudal lord.

The crop yields were not high compared to those achieved by modern farming methods and a poor harvest led to food shortages and sometimes famine.

By the 13th century, the most profitable agricultural product was wool. Much of England's wealth was built upon the wool trade. Some areas of the country, especially the north and west, were ideally suited to sheep farming. In these regions, local industries developed in processing the fleeces before they were taken for sale in the markets and fairs.

Peasants also kept animals. A peasant might have one or two cows for milking and some sheep. These could be grazed on common land and would be put on the freshly harvested fields to eat the roots of the crops. Pigs were driven into the woods to eat acorns and bark. This was a right for freemen but villeins had to pay to do this. At night, animals were either brought into the house or put into stalls to keep them safe from wild animals. Keeping animals well fed during the winter was difficult and the amount of milk produced by the cows declined significantly during these months.

Peasant life

Peasants lived in small houses with thatched roofs known as cruck houses. The walls were made of wooden strips woven together and then plastered with manure. This was known as wattle and daub. They would have just one room to live in and very little furniture. The floors would be covered with straw that could be changed when it became too dirty. They would very likely have been cold in the winter and hot in the summer.

Peasant labour

Life was hard for a medieval peasant. Work began at dawn and lasted till dusk. The work carried out depended on the season; in the spring the fields were sown with crops, in the summer the crops were harvested and in the autumn the fields were ploughed in preparation for the next crop. The tools used were basic, which made the work physically demanding.

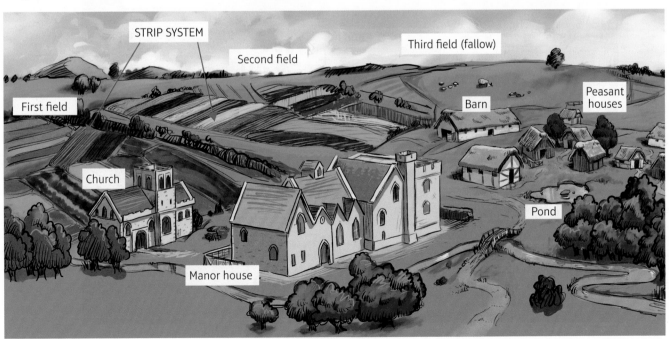

Figure 1.8 A manorial estate showing the three-field farming system.

Peasant women and children

The lives of most medieval women were controlled by men, firstly by their father and then by their husband. When a woman married she became the property of her husband and her life revolved around caring for his needs. For a medieval peasant woman this meant that her main role was carrying out domestic duties. This included caring for the children, cooking, and spinning and weaving. She grew food in a vegetable garden and looked after small animals like chickens and geese. She was expected to provide basic nursing for her family, so many women developed an understanding of the use of herbs in making simple medicines.

A peasant woman would also have had duties on the land, especially at harvest time when she would help to bring in the crop. A daughter would be expected to help her mother with the household and farm duties in preparation for when she married.

The children of peasants did not go to school. As soon as they were old enough, they joined their father in the fields. Although they could not carry out the hard labouring tasks, they could clear the fields of stones and scare away the birds. As they grew older and stronger they would be able to take on more physically demanding roles.

Rural pastimes

Rural life was not completely focused on work. There were occasions for merry-making. These were often connected to pagan (pre-Christian) or Christian festivals. On these days the villagers gathered on the village green and enjoyed sports like wrestling. All festivals were accompanied by ale-drinking, with the highest honours going to the man who could empty the largest tankard (mug). However, ale was expensive, so the medieval peasant could not indulge himself very often.

Towns and town life

The 12th century was a golden period for the development of towns in the Middle Ages. Old towns grew and new towns were founded as a result of increasing trade. However, most towns would have been only a little different from villages in their appearance and farming activities would still have taken place within their walls.

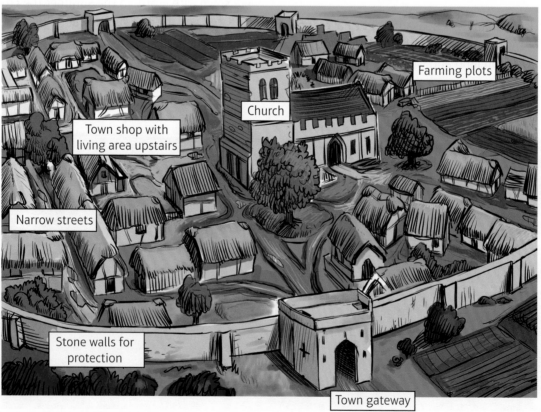

Figure 1.9 The main features of a medieval town.

Town government

Many of the towns were established by a royal charter. This charter granted the town its freedom from the control of the local lord. A town had a law court and had a form of self-government. Both Richard and John granted the charters in return for the payment of large sums of money. The charters granted the citizens freedoms from certain taxes.

London was the biggest town. It had elected officials, called aldermen, who played important roles in governing the city and in law courts. Each alderman was responsible for an area of London called a ward. Twelve of them sat in the law courts and made judgements on legal cases. The people of London were given more freedom in town government when, in 1215, John allowed them to elect their own mayor to govern the city.

Town guilds

Guilds developed out of groups of individuals working in the same trade. For example, the guild records from Leicester show a wide range of different guilds including weavers, dyers, goldsmiths, bakers, carpenters and masons. There were 40 towns with guilds by the end of John's reign. Members had to pay an entrance fee and give a guarantee that they would pay their taxes.

Membership of a guild meant that a tradesman had an unrestricted right to trade in the town. If you were not a member, you could not practise that trade. The most important guilds by the end of the 12th century were those associated with the manufacture of cloth because wool production was England's richest industry. English cloth was sold across Europe – mainly to the Low Countries (modern day Belgium and the Netherlands).

The role of towns in the economy

Towns played an essential role in trade and in raising revenue for the king.

- Trade was controlled by tolls, which had to be paid on sales and purchases. Tolls were also collected when people used certain roads and bridges, and to pass through town gates. Both Richard and John also collected customs duties, which were taxes on goods that were imported and exported.

- Buying and selling was often carried out in local markets, which were usually held on a Sunday. Traders sold goods on open tables or stalls and sales records were kept. Officials collected rents for the tables and stalls and also charged for the use of official weights and measures. Market trade boosted a town's income and allowed some towns to become very wealthy.

- Trade required the building of roads and bridges. Town governments became responsible for maintaining the roads in and around their towns. However, roads flooded and bridges often collapsed, making travel slow and difficult, which affected trade.

- Large towns with ports were crucial to England's trade as they enabled goods to be bought from, and sold to, foreign countries. They also helped speed up trade between coastal towns in England as it was quicker to travel by sea than by road.

Annual fairs

Some towns hosted annual fairs. They were usually held on important days in the Christian calendar. Fairs usually lasted several days and attracted traders from other towns and even foreign countries. The first purpose was merry-making; this might involve sports like archery, bowling and skittles, and the taverns and stalls would sell mead (an alcoholic drink made from honey) and ale. Afterwards, important trade was carried out. This included trading luxury goods like wines and silks. Towns paid for a king's licence to hold a fair, and fairs raised huge amounts of money in taxes and tolls.

Life in a town

One key difference in comparison to the countryside was that all townsmen were free. Indeed, if a villein ran away from his village and lived in a town for a year and a day without being caught, he became a freeman. This meant he was free to choose the work he did rather than being tied to the land as a labourer.

> **Activity**   **?**
>
> Read pages 30–34. Write a diary entry for a day in the life of a peasant or town dweller. You will need to outline their responsibilities and say what they do in their spare time.

Unlike in the countryside, the population of the towns were employed in many different jobs. For example, people became blacksmiths, butchers, weavers and builders. These jobs required training and so young people were apprenticed to a master craftsman from the age of 14. They were trained for between five and nine years before they could practise the trade themselves, and only if they belonged to the guild. An apprenticeship was a desirable position and parents paid the master to train their child. In the towns there was the opportunity for children to work in a different occupation to their parents, but in the countryside, the child of a villein would be raised to work on the land.

The life of a woman was, in some ways, different in the town compared to the countryside. A woman still had her domestic duties to fulfil but she might also work in a trade. Many women supported their husbands, for example, in a bakery or serving in a tavern, or in a skilled occupation, like weaving. Some women were allowed to join guilds, although this was less usual. A widow might join the guild to run her late husband's business.

The towns themselves were crowded and dirty. Town inhabitants emptied chamber pots into the streets and rain washed this waste into the wells, causing disease. Wooden houses were built on narrow streets, often with shops at the front. The streets began to fill with people from early morning (around 5 a.m.). Most shops opened at 6 a.m. and stayed open until 3 p.m., but some continued their business until around 9 p.m. When night fell, the town watchmen patrolled the walls to keep the people safe from attackers and from accidental fires that could spread rapidly in the narrow streets of wooden houses. All towns were separated from the countryside by strong stone walls that protected the population and their wealth (see Source B). Traders could be charged tolls at the gates.

Jews in medieval England

The Jews were a separate community in medieval England. Jews had no country of their own and had settled in towns across Europe. However, because they were not Christian, they were outcasts from society and were always under threat of attack by Christians.

The legal status of the Jews

The number of Jews in England had begun to grow from 1150. By 1200, there were about 5,000 Jews in England. They had settled in large towns like London, York and Norwich. They were allowed to live in England under the protection of the king. This right was confirmed by John by charter in 1201. Under the charter, the Jews did not have to pay tolls and customs duties, and their rights of inheritance were guaranteed. However, these freedoms did not come cheaply. The Jews were the property of the king and he could tax them whenever he wanted.

Source B

The medieval town walls of the city of York as they stand today. York was a prosperous medieval town and these early 13th-century walls protected its inhabitants.

The Jews' role in money lending

Christians were not allowed to charge interest* for lending money (known as 'usury'), but Jews were. Therefore money lending became their main business, especially as they were banned from many other occupations. Their role in money lending became an essential part of the medieval economy. Huge amounts of money were owed to the Jews. For example, Aaron of Lincoln was owed so much money that a separate 'exchequer'* had to be set up to deal with the debts owed to him after his death.

The death of a Jewish money lender could be very profitable for the king. In 1194, a law was passed that registered all debts owed to the Jews. If a Jewish money lender died without making a will, the king had the right to collect the debts owed to him.

Key terms

Interest*

An additional payment to be made to a money lender as the price for borrowing money. It is usually a percentage of the total loan.

Exchequer*

A royal counting house where coins were counted and weighed. It was called the exchequer after the chequered cloth that was used to assist in the counting.

The pogroms of 1189–90

Causes

On some occasions, there were violent attacks on the Jewish population known as **pogroms**. The underlying cause of the pogroms was anti-Semitism*:

- Christians regarded money lending as unchristian, but at the same time many were angry because it enabled some Jews to become wealthy.
- Jews were accused of being the 'Christ killers' because, according to the Bible, they had condemned Jesus to die on the cross.

The trigger for the pogroms of 1189–90 was an incident at Richard's coronation. The Jews of London decided to present Richard with a gift. However, some Christians in the crowd thought that this was an insult to the new king. A riot started and Christians began killing Jews.

Key term

Anti-Semitism*

Hatred or discrimination against Jews.

The slaughter spread across London and the houses of Jews were burned down. Richard was furious. The Jews were under his protection and their wealth was too valuable to him to allow such attacks. He hanged the ringleaders and sent orders to every shire that the Jews were not to be harmed.

The extent of the pogrom

In spite of Richard's orders, the frenzy of killing swept across the country over the next few months. In East Anglia, Jews were slaughtered in Norwich and King's Lynn, before the pogrom continued northwards to Lincoln and, by March 1190, York. Here, when the mob began killing Jews, 150 of them took refuge in Clifford's Tower, the castle in York. However, with no way out, the men killed their wives and children, and then committed suicide. Any survivors were killed by the mob.

The Jewish community did survive the pogrom, but it marked a decline in their prosperity. The massacre of Jews was regarded as acceptable by many Christians at the time. In Source C, the chronicler Richard of Devizes uses language in his account that shows he believed that the killing was justified.

Source C

Richard of Devizes was a monk from Winchester and in 1192 he wrote the *Chronicle of the deeds of Richard I*. Here he calls the massacre of the Jews after Richard's coronation a sacrifice to the devil (who he believed the Jews worshipped).

[In] 1189, Richard... was consecrated king of the English by Baldwin, Archbishop of Canterbury, at Westminster. On the very day of the coronation... a sacrifice of the Jews to their father, the devil, was commenced in the city of London, and so long was the duration of this famous mystery [religious ritual] that the holocaust [religious sacrifice] could scarcely be accomplished the ensuing [following] day. The other cities and towns of the kingdom emulated [copied] the faith of the Londoners, and with a like devotion dispatched their bloodsuckers with blood to hell.

Interpretation 1

Frank McLynn explains the hatred for the Jews at the time of Richard's coronation in his book *Lionheart and Lackland: King Richard, King John and the Wars of Conquest* (2006).

Some of London's wealthier Jews, eager to establish themselves with the new king, arrived bearing gifts. Somehow the Christian crowds at the gate got it into their heads that this was a[n]… insult to the newly crowned king; this was, after all, an era, in which the Jews were doubly execrated [loathed] – for being the killers of Christ and for usury, defined in church law as the lending of money at interest… Moreover, Jews were loathed for… the ostentatious [showy] wealth that a few of them… liked to display. Additionally, they were widely believed to murder Christian children for ritual purposes… There were also many great aristocratic families [and] abbeys… in debt to Jewish money lenders, people who would shed no tears if their debts were… wiped out by the death of their creditors [the Jews they owned money to].

Royal exploitation of the Jews through taxation

Both Richard and John needed the Jews for the taxes that they paid and for the money that they loaned. For example, in 1194, the Jews were required to pay £3,375 towards Richard's ransom.

Although John granted the Jewish community its rights by charter in 1201 (see page 34), this came at the cost of £2,700. In 1207, he became even more demanding on the Jews.

- John demanded a tallage of £2,700.
- John demanded one tenth of the value of all their loans. This also hit Christians hard when John began to demand swift repayment of the loans.

Still being short of money, John went even further in 1210. He began arresting Jews and demanded that the Jewish community pay a tallage of £44,000. Every Jew, even the very poorest, were expected to contribute to the tallage. Some historians claim that it took the Jews a decade to recover financially from this demand.

Summary

- Most of England's population were peasants who lived and worked on their lord's land. The majority of rural work involved growing crops, but peasants also raised animals.
- The number of towns was increasing. Some were established by a charter and had their own form of government. Guilds controlled the people working in different occupations.
- Towns were important centres of trade, which was often conducted through markets and fairs. Trade provided an income for the king through the payment of taxes and tolls.
- The Jews were a separate community in England with royal protection. Some Jews grew rich through the practice of money lending. They were often the target of anti-Semitism, and sometimes, pogroms.

Checkpoint

Strengthen

S1 Draw a table with two columns. Head one column 'Town' and the other one 'Countryside'.
In the correct column, list the activities carried out by the populations of these areas.

S2 Give two reasons why the Jews were hated by many Christians at the end of the 12th century.

Challenge

C1 Compare the lives of women and children in the towns and the countryside and explain how they are different.

C2 Why did Richard and John protect the status of the Jews? Explain your answer.

How confident do you feel about your answers to these questions? If you are not sure you answered them well, try planning your answers before writing them.

Recap: Life and government in England, 1189–1216

Recall quiz

1 What was the feudal system?
2 What was knight's service?
3 What was a villein?
4 What is primogeniture?
5 List two promises that the king made in his coronation oath.
6 Who did Richard put in charge of England's government while he was absent on crusade?
7 Give two reasons why King John murdered his nephew, Prince Arthur.
8 List three factors that made John an unpopular king.
9 What is scutage?
10 List three ways in which towns played a role in raising revenues from trade.

Activities

1 Describe two different types of tax that were collected in the years 1189–1216.
2 The 13th-century chronicler, Matthew Paris, wrote that hell was too good for John. Make a list of the evidence from this chapter that would agree with Paris' opinion of John.
3 Create two concept maps (spider diagrams), one with 'countryside' at the centre and the other with 'towns' at the centre. On each concept map draw 'branches' from the main topic to important features of life in the towns and the countryside.
4 Link the features that are similar for life in the towns and countryside on the concept maps by drawing arrows between them of the same colour.

Exam-style question, Section B

'The main difference between life in medieval towns and villages was that town dwellers were free'.

How far do you agree? Explain your answer.

You may use the following in your answer:

- the villein
- the guilds.

You **must** also use information of your own. **16 marks**

Exam tip

This question is about comparison. You should identify three features that were different in the town and countryside. Give some details to explain in what way the features were similar or different. Try to explain which feature had the greatest difference.

Writing historically: managing sentences

The most successful historical writing is clearly expressed, using carefully managed sentence structures.

Learning outcomes

By the end of this lesson, you will understand how to:

- select and use single clause and multiple clause sentences.

Definitions

Clause: a group of words or unit of meaning that contains a verb and can form part or all of a sentence, e.g. 'Richard I ruled England from 1189'.

Single clause sentence: a sentence containing just one clause, e.g. 'Richard I went on crusade'.

Multiple clause sentence: a sentence containing two or more clauses, often linked with a conjunction, e.g. 'Richard I went on crusade and left England for five years'.

Coordinating conjunction: a word used to link two clauses of equal importance within a sentence, e.g. 'and', 'but', 'so', 'or', etc.

How can I structure my sentences clearly?

When you are explaining and exploring complex events and ideas, you can end up writing very long sentences. These can make your writing difficult for the reader to follow.

Look at the extract below from a response to this exam-style question:

> Describe **two** features of kingship at the end of the 12th century. **(4 marks)**

> A medieval king needed to be strong and keep his kingdom safe and Richard I was a great warrior who successfully defended his lands but John was not yet they were both anointed with holy oils so people knew that God had chosen them.

1. The writer of the response above has linked every piece of information in his answer into one, very long sentence.

   How many different pieces of information has the writer included in this answer? Rewrite each piece of information as a **single clause sentence**. For example:

   > Richard I was a great warrior who successfully defended his lands.

2. Look again at your answer to Question 1. Which of the single clause sentences would you link together? Rewrite the response twice, experimenting with linking different sentences together using **coordinating conjunctions** such as 'and', 'but' or 'so'. Remember: you are aiming to make your writing as clear and precise as possible.

3. Write three two-clause sentences, using conjunctions, on the topic of kingship at the end of the 12th century.

4. Now rewrite your response to Question 3. Experiment with linking different sentences together using conjunctions such as 'and', 'but' or 'so'. Remember: you are aiming to make your writing as clear and precise as possible.

How can I use conjunctions to link my ideas?

There are several types of **multiple clause sentence** structures that you can use to link your ideas.

If you want to balance or contrast two ideas of equal importance within a sentence, you can use coordinating conjunctions to link them.

Look at the extract below from a response to this exam-style question:

> Explain why Richard became king in 1189. **(12 marks)**

> Richard was Henry II's eldest living legitimate son. He was Eleanor's favourite and Duke of Aquitaine and more powerful than John. This not only made Richard the only realistic candidate but also made John realise he had no chance of rivalling him. In the end John supported Richard not because it was right but because he understood he was outmatched and accepted the need to win favour with the soon-to-be king.

These coordinating conjunctions link equally important actions that happened at the same time.

These paired coordinating conjunctions contrast two possible causes.

These paired coordinating conjunctions link and balance two equally important ideas.

5. How else could the writer of the response above have linked, balanced or contrasted these ideas? Experiment with rewriting the response, using different sentence structures and different ways of linking ideas within them using coordinating conjunctions.

Did you notice?

The first sentence in the response above is a single clause sentence, containing one verb:

> Richard was Henry II's eldest living legitimate son.

6. Why do you think the writer chose to give this point additional emphasis by structuring it as a short, single clause sentence? Write a sentence or two explaining your ideas.

Improving an answer

7. Now look at the final paragraph, below, of the response to the exam-style question above.

> Richard I was the first English king for over 100 years to succeed his father. He had to fight against his father to defend his inheritance. His younger brother, John, was Henry II's favourite. Richard was supported by his mother. The Duchy of Aquitaine brought Richard wealth and power. John had no lands in 1189. John could not rival the strength of Richard's position or claim.

Rewrite this paragraph, choosing some conjunctions from the **Coordinating Conjunction Bank** below to link, balance or contrast the writer's ideas.

Coordinating Conjunction Bank

and	not only… but
but	also…
or	either… or…
so	neither… nor
	both… and…

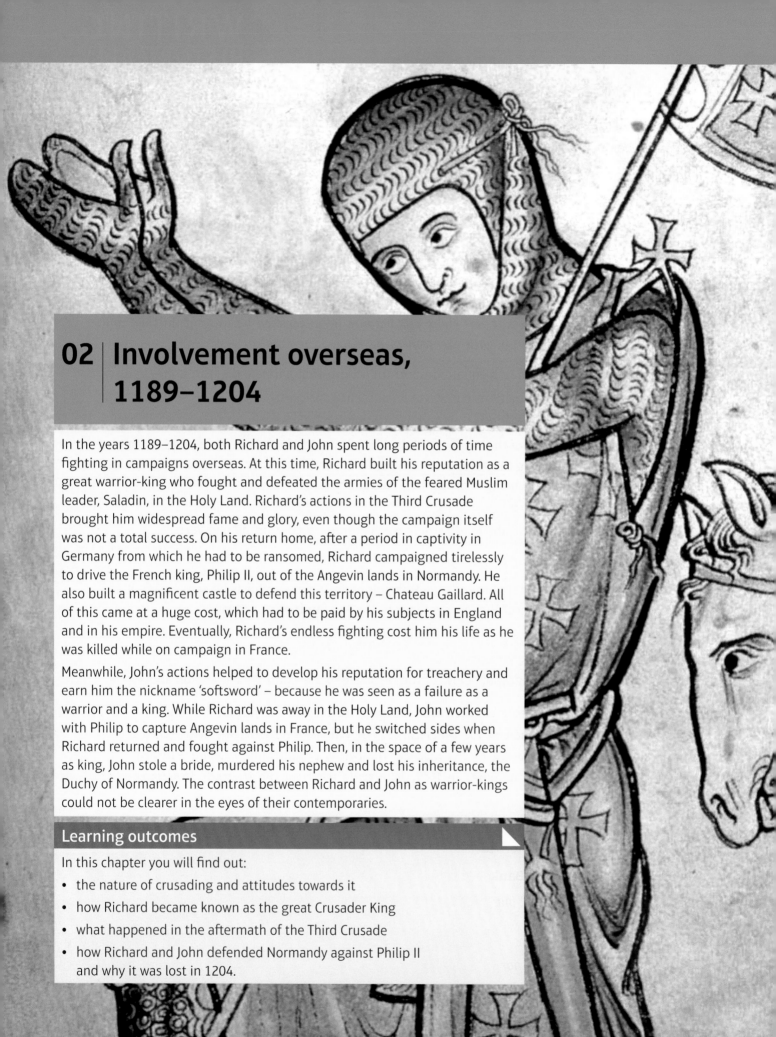

02 | Involvement overseas, 1189–1204

In the years 1189–1204, both Richard and John spent long periods of time fighting in campaigns overseas. At this time, Richard built his reputation as a great warrior-king who fought and defeated the armies of the feared Muslim leader, Saladin, in the Holy Land. Richard's actions in the Third Crusade brought him widespread fame and glory, even though the campaign itself was not a total success. On his return home, after a period in captivity in Germany from which he had to be ransomed, Richard campaigned tirelessly to drive the French king, Philip II, out of the Angevin lands in Normandy. He also built a magnificent castle to defend this territory – Chateau Gaillard. All of this came at a huge cost, which had to be paid by his subjects in England and in his empire. Eventually, Richard's endless fighting cost him his life as he was killed while on campaign in France.

Meanwhile, John's actions helped to develop his reputation for treachery and earn him the nickname 'softsword' – because he was seen as a failure as a warrior and a king. While Richard was away in the Holy Land, John worked with Philip to capture Angevin lands in France, but he switched sides when Richard returned and fought against Philip. Then, in the space of a few years as king, John stole a bride, murdered his nephew and lost his inheritance, the Duchy of Normandy. The contrast between Richard and John as warrior-kings could not be clearer in the eyes of their contemporaries.

Learning outcomes

In this chapter you will find out:

- the nature of crusading and attitudes towards it
- how Richard became known as the great Crusader King
- what happened in the aftermath of the Third Crusade
- how Richard and John defended Normandy against Philip II and why it was lost in 1204.

2.1 The nature of crusading

The concept of crusade

A crusade was a holy war fought by Christians. At this time, the main objective of a crusade was to restore the Holy Land, especially Jerusalem, to Christian control. By 1095, these lands had fallen into the hands of the Seljuk Turks. The Seljuk Turks were Muslims and the Christians were hostile to them because of their different faith. In 1095, the pope called upon Christians to rescue Jerusalem and the Holy Land. In other words, he called for a crusade against the Seljuk Turks. This was known as the First Crusade.

In principle, the Christian Church was against violence, but it was never pacifist, and it developed teachings to explain the circumstances in which Christians could fight a war:

- a war was allowed if it was called by a legitimate authority, like a king or a bishop
- a war needed a just cause
- a war should be fought with the minimum of violence.

Under these circumstances, the war would be a '**just war**'. However, there was still a problem that violence was sinful and could condemn a man to hell. To prevent this, a man who took part in war had to seek forgiveness and do penance* for his sins. This penance could be set aside if the man was granted something called an indulgence*.

To encourage knights to join the First Crusade the pope promised participants a **full indulgence** that would grant them salvation (direct entry to heaven) when they died – they would not have to go to purgatory*. The promise of salvation persuaded many knights in Europe to go on crusade and it was repeated each time a pope called for a crusade. Although the First Crusade achieved its aim with the capture of Jerusalem, the Holy City was not secure. In 1187, Jerusalem fell to Muslim forces. A new crusade was needed to reclaim it.

Extend your knowledge

Purgatory and the role of indulgences

The Catholic Church teaches that entry into heaven is not automatic. Catholics are expected to confess their sins to a priest regularly and to do penance for them. However, if they die with their sins unconfessed or for which they have not done proper penance, they cannot enter directly into heaven. Instead they must undergo a period of purgatory – a state in which they are 'purged' of their sins and are cut off from God until they are purified.

Key terms

Penance*

A punishment inflicted on oneself to show repentance of wrongdoing or sins.

Indulgence*

A kind of pardon given by the Catholic Church that reduces the amount of penance a sinner must perform in life or in purgatory after death. A full indulgence would grant someone direct entry into heaven when they died.

Purgatory*

A state of existence, according to Catholic teaching, where people are 'purged' of their sins after they die. This purifies them so that they can enter heaven.

A 13th-century map of the world showing Jerusalem at the centre. This shows how important Jerusalem was to medieval Christians.

The immediate causes of the Third Crusade

After the First Crusade, four crusader states were established by the Christians. However, these four states were surrounded by enemies and very vulnerable to attack. The states were also weakened by constant bickering and jealousy between the main Christian lords ruling them. These weaknesses were ruthlessly exploited by a powerful Muslim leader, Saladin, who had united the Muslims in the region. In July 1187, Saladin defeated the main Christian army in the Battle of Hattin. He then attacked Jerusalem, which fell under his control in October 1187.

Pope Gregory VIII was shocked when the news reached Europe about the fall of Jerusalem. He issued a papal bull* (see Source B) in which he described the horrors of the treatment of Christians at the hands of the Muslims. He called upon Christians to launch a new crusade (known as the Third Crusade) and offered a full indulgence for anyone who died on crusade.

Key term

Papal bull*

An official letter or declaration made by the pope.

Source B

An extract from the papal bull issued by Pope Gregory VIII on 29 October 1187.

On hearing with what severe and terrible judgement the land of Jerusalem has been struck by the divine hand, we and our brothers have been stunned by such great horror and affected by such great sorrow that we could not easily decide what to do or say. Faced with such distress concerning that land, moreover, we ought to consider not only the sins of its inhabitants but also our own and those of the whole Christian people. It is therefore necessary for all of us to amend our sins with penance and good works. To those who undertake the journey [go on crusade] and die in penitence for their sins, we promise full indulgence of their faults and eternal life.

Extend your knowledge

Saladin

Saladin was the ruler of Egypt and Syria. He was an expert horseman and considered to be a man of good grace and honour. He aimed to defend Islam and unify the Muslim world against the Christian invaders. His capture of Jerusalem was celebrated by Muslims and many regarded him as a hero. He treated the Christians in Jerusalem with mercy and allowed most of them to leave unharmed on payment of a ransom. However, the defeat of the Christians at the Battle of Hattin and at Jerusalem in 1187 meant that his reputation at the time amongst Christians in Europe was that of an evil monster.

The English crusading army

The English crusading army was one of three armies that left for the Holy Land in 1190. The other two armies were led by Frederick I (usually known as Barbarossa, because of his red beard), the Holy Roman Emperor*, and Philip II, the king of France.

Key term

Holy Roman Emperor*

The head of the Holy Roman Empire – an empire that consisted of different states in areas of Europe that are now largely in Germany and Italy.

In total, Richard gathered a force of approximately 17,000 men in Sicily in 1191. These men came from England and the Angevin Empire.

Who were the English crusaders?

The majority of the English crusaders were knights and their military households. The military household would include the knights' squires, who were their servants and in training to become knights. The members of the military household would have outnumbered the knights on the crusade.

Among the English crusader knights were men of high rank, such as the earls of Leicester and Ferrers. As a whole, the army was highly disciplined and professional. Most knights were experienced fighters.

In addition to the knights and their military households, Richard's army included:

• Roger of Howden, a royal clerk who spent one year on crusade and recorded the experience in his chronicle of the deeds of Richard I.

Source C

This image from the 12th-century *Westminster Psalter* shows a crusader knight at prayer in front of his horse.

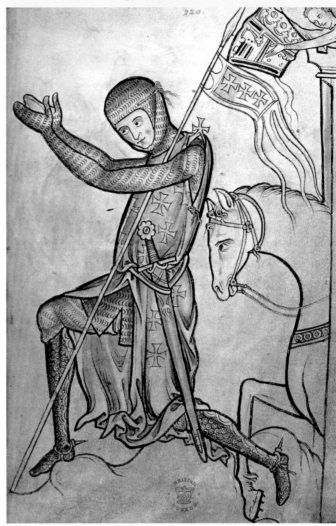

• Leading churchmen including Baldwin (the Archbishop of Canterbury), who was sent to the Holy Land before the crusading army, and Hubert Walter (the bishop of Salisbury).

• Nearly 3,000 Welsh archers volunteered to accompany the crusade, although the delay in setting off meant that considerably fewer actually left for the Holy Land. These bowmen were highly skilled professionals who fought with longbows.

• Thousands of camp followers – civilians who took care of essential tasks for the army, like cooking and nursing. Some were the wives of the crusaders.

Why did men join the crusade?

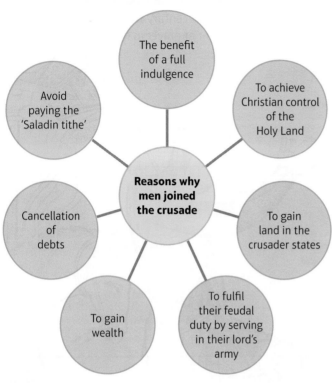

Figure 2.1 A summary of reasons why men joined the crusade.

The first and most important reason for joining the crusade was religious. Men responded to Pope Gregory's call to defend the holy places and win back Jerusalem for the Christians. They were also attracted by the indulgence that promised forgiveness of sins and entry to heaven. Other churchmen, like Archbishop Baldwin, also played their part in recruiting volunteers. Baldwin spent a year touring Wales encouraging men to 'take the cross'*. He was said to have enlisted 3,000 crusaders.

Key term

Take the cross*

Christians who took the vow to go on crusade promised to 'take the cross'. The sign of the crusade was a cross.

However, there were other more immediate benefits of going on crusade. The principle of primogeniture meant that fiefs in England and the Angevin Empire were inherited by the eldest son. Younger sons joined the crusade in the hope that they would win land in the crusader states.

There were other financial benefits to going on the crusade. Crusaders were promised that their debts would be cancelled. In addition, they did not have to pay the '**Saladin tithe**' (a tithe is a tax) that was collected to fund the crusade. There was also a chance that they might gain some wealth in the Holy Land from ransoms or loot.

Many knights joined the crusade when their feudal overlord joined as part of their knight service (see page 10). They tended to travel in bands with knights from the same area. Joining a crusade allowed them to demonstrate their military skills and chivalric values. The full indulgence from the pope also meant that they would not be sinning by fighting a war.

Source D

A heroic account of Archbishop Baldwin's role in the Third Crusade as described by Gerald of Wales in his *Journey through Wales*. Gerald was a clergyman and a royal clerk who accompanied Archbishop Baldwin on his tour of Wales in 1188, where Baldwin encouraged men to join the crusade.

Archbishop Baldwin, having heard of the insults offered to our Saviour and his holy cross [the defeat of the Christians in 1187], was amongst the first who took the cross, and preached the crusade both at home and in the most remote parts of the kingdom. Pursuing his journey to the Holy Land, he boarded a ship at Marseilles, and landed safely in a port at Tyre, from where he proceeded to Acre. Here he found our army both attacking and attacked, and thrown into a state of despair. As his death approached, he embraced his fellow subjects and provided charity to relieve their wants. His life and actions strengthened them in the faith.

Activity ?

Why did men join the crusade? Draw a table with two columns. Label one side 'religious reasons' and the other side 'other reasons'. Working together with a partner, decide which reasons to write in each column.

Attitudes in England to the crusaders

It seems clear that most English people supported the call for a crusade. It was considered a godly act for crusaders to journey to the Holy Land and fight for Christianity. Going on a pilgrimage* was common at this time, and it was a key part of English religious life and culture. The most important holy site for pilgrims was Jerusalem and it had been easier for English pilgrims to make the long journey there while it was under Christian control. So, people in England were horrified when Jerusalem had fallen back into Muslim hands in 1187 and felt an obligation to support the crusade.

The positive attitude of the English towards crusading is clearly shown by the reputation that Richard the Lionheart gained as a great king, which in large part was due to his role in the Third Crusade. Richard was seen as a defender of the Christian faith by people at the time and taking part in a crusade was considered the highest duty that any king could perform.

The support for the crusade was also demonstrated in the slaughter of the Jews in the pogrom of 1189–90 (see page 35). The massacre was not only prompted by resentment of Jewish wealth from money lending, but on religious grounds. Denounced as the 'killers of Christ', the Jews were seen as the ultimate enemy by many Christians. As Interpretation 1 explains, the crusading atmosphere of 1189–90 was an important reason for the attack on the Jews.

Key term
Pilgrimage*
A journey made for religious reasons to a designated holy place, often as a form of penance.

Interpretation 1

An explanation of the motivation for the attack on the Jews in 1189–90 from *Lionheart and Lackland: King Richard, King John and the Wars of Conquest* (2006) by Frank McLynn.

It was difficult to convince the Crusade-happy mob that Jews should be left alone. If Muslims were to be slaughtered by European armies occupying the Holy Places in Jerusalem, how much more deserving of death were the people who actually crucified the Saviour. It was this kind of fanatical feeling that lay behind the anti-Semitic riots.

Exam-style question, Section B

'The main reason why most people supported the Third Crusade was because they wanted to restore Christian control in the Holy Land'. How far do you agree? Explain your answer.

You may use the following in your answer:

- Pope Gregory VIII
- the 'Saladin tithe'.

You **must** also use information of your own.   **16 marks**

Exam tip

When explaining the reasons why something happened, you should identify at least three reasons and write a sentence to explain how each reason led to the outcome. A good answer will make links between the reasons and show why one reason was most important.

However, despite the crusading fervour, there were some concerns.

- Family members would have to manage lands for the absent knight. Since sons often accompanied the father on crusade, decisions had to be made about who would stay and who would go.
- The cost of the crusade was resented. The 'Saladin tithe' and, later, the cost of Richard's ransom (see page 56) put a further financial burden on the already heavily-taxed population. Many took the cross to avoid paying the 'Saladin tithe' – showing its unpopularity.
- One English chronicler, William of Newburgh, criticised Richard's decision to go on crusade. He argued that a king of England should be present

in his country. While William of Newburgh was the only chronicler who complained openly, it is likely that others in England had similar concerns about Richard's decision to embark on a long, dangerous journey to a distant land.

Activities

1 In pairs, write a list of reasons why people in England might have supported the Third Crusade and another list of reasons why they might not.
2 Still in pairs, rank each list in order of importance.
3 Organise a class debate. One half of the class should argue in favour of the crusade and the other half should argue against it. Make a note of the best points made in the debate.

Summary

- A crusade was a holy war declared by Christians against non-Christians. In this period they were focused on restoring Christian control of Jerusalem and the Holy Land.
- Christians who joined the crusade were granted an indulgence for the forgiveness of sins and immediate entry to heaven when they died. A crusade was seen as a 'just war'.
- The Third Crusade was declared by Pope Gregory VIII after Jerusalem fell to the control of Muslims led by Saladin in 1187.
- Richard the Lionheart led an army of 17,000 men on crusade. It included leading noblemen, hundreds of knights, churchmen and Welsh archers.
- Most English people supported the crusade, but they did have some concerns and its cost was resented.

Checkpoint

Strengthen

S1 How many armies departed for the Holy Land in 1190 and who were the leaders?

S2 Describe the different types of people who went on crusade.

S3 Sum up in a paragraph the English attitude to the Third Crusade.

Challenge

C1 In what ways was a knight's decision to go on crusade linked to his role in the feudal system? Consider the following: primogeniture, the chivalric code, knight service. It might help to look back at Chapter 1 to refresh your knowledge of the feudal system.

C2 Explain the benefits of joining the Third Crusade and why they caused many people to take the cross.

How confident do you feel about your answers to these questions? If you are not sure you answered them well, try sharing your answers with a partner and see if you can improve them together.

2.2 Richard, the Crusader King

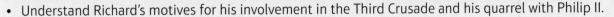

Learning outcomes

- Understand Richard's motives for his involvement in the Third Crusade and his quarrel with Philip II.
- Understand Richard's victories at Acre and Arsuf.
- Understand the reasons for Richard's failure to capture Jerusalem.

Richard took the cross in the autumn of 1187, 18 months before he became king of England. As soon as he had been crowned in September 1189, he began his preparations for the crusade. He left England in December 1189.

Richard's motives for going on crusade

Richard was the first western prince to take the cross in 1187. His decision to take part was celebrated by troubadours*, who believed that Richard would inspire other princes and nobles to follow his example and join the crusade.

There are a number of factors that motivated Richard to go on crusade in 1190, see Figure 2.2.

Key term

Troubadour*

A writer and performer of songs and poems that glorified chivalry and warfare.

Personal connections – I am the great grandson of Fulk of Anjou, who had been king of Jerusalem. Fighting in the Holy Land is in my blood.

Personal glory – This is a chance to be remembered as a great warrior, celebrated in the songs and poems of the troubadours.

Religious devotion – The crusade is the sacred duty of good Christians.

Opportunity – Now that I am king, I have all the wealth and power that I need to go on crusade. There will never be a better time.

Figure 2.2 Richard's motivations to go on crusade.

Richard's quarrel with Philip II

Richard and Philip II of France departed on crusade at the same time. Even before they left on crusade, there was bad feeling between the two kings.

- Philip wanted to extend the royal lands in France by taking lands from the Angevin Empire.
- Richard held a strategically important strip of land in France, called the Vexin, as the dowry for marrying Philip's sister Alice, but Richard had not married her.

Timeline

Richard I and the Third Crusade

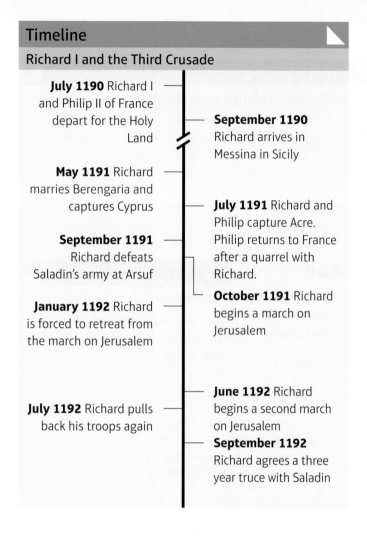

July 1190 Richard I and Philip II of France depart for the Holy Land

September 1190 Richard arrives in Messina in Sicily

May 1191 Richard marries Berengaria and captures Cyprus

July 1191 Richard and Philip capture Acre. Philip returns to France after a quarrel with Richard.

September 1191 Richard defeats Saladin's army at Arsuf

October 1191 Richard begins a march on Jerusalem

January 1192 Richard is forced to retreat from the march on Jerusalem

June 1192 Richard begins a second march on Jerusalem

July 1192 Richard pulls back his troops again

September 1192 Richard agrees a three year truce with Saladin

The two kings agreed that, if they went on crusade together, neither would be able to attack the other's lands. This meant that their quarrels would be suspended for the duration of the crusade. However, things did not work out as they had intended.

The crusade got off to a bad start for the leaders. Frederick Barbarossa was the most important of the European rulers who joined the crusade. He led an army of 15,000 soldiers. However, Frederick drowned in June 1190 crossing a river in Turkey and many of his troops returned home. The loss of Frederick increased the rivalry between Richard and Philip as each man competed for the role as the leader of the crusade.

The first problem arose in Messina in Sicily. Both kings arrived there, but, unlike Philip, Richard was given a magnificent reception by the Sicilians. This made Philip jealous and he announced that he would depart for the Holy Land immediately. However, the seas were rough and he was forced to return. This was another humiliation.

The next problem arose when Richard landed in Cyprus. While in Cyprus, Richard married Berengaria of Navarre. Richard had arranged his engagement to Berengaria before Philip took the crusader vows, but had kept this quiet to prevent a war. Although Philip agreed to release Richard from his planned marriage to Alice, he was still angered and humiliated by Richard's actions.

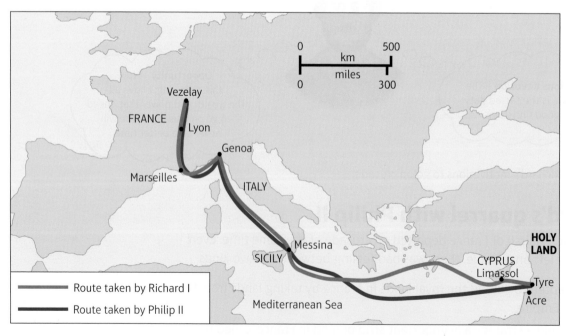

Figure 2.3 A map showing the routes taken by Richard I and Philip II during the Third Crusade.

The quarrel became much worse because Richard did not just land on Cyprus, he conquered it. Philip believed that he was entitled to half of the value of Cyprus because, in July 1190, he and Richard had agreed to divide their conquests equally. Richard refused as Philip had played no part in its conquest. The victory was of great importance to Richard. Not only was he able to sell the island for 100,000 gold coins but he gained control of the island's grain, which secured an important supply of food for the crusaders.

Extend your knowledge

Philip II
Philip II ruled France from the age of 16. His greatest ambition was to expand his territory and assert his power over his vassals, particularly the Angevins. He had already had some success in manipulating the rivalries between Henry II and his sons before Richard became king, though without yet having gained any of the territory he wanted.

Philip put aside his differences with Richard when he took the cross. However, the chances of maintaining a good relationship were slim, even from the outset. Philip recruited a smaller army than Richard and it was not as well equipped. This reflects the different levels of wealth that each man could muster to support the crusade. Philip's lands were smaller and provided less income for its king. This irritated Philip.

Further problems arose at Acre in July 1191. Although Richard and Philip won a joint victory at Acre (see page 50), their squabbling continued. Philip was angry that Richard had used his wealth to pay his soldiers higher wages than Philip could afford to pay his men. There was also a dispute over who should be king of Jerusalem: Richard favoured the claim of Guy de Lusignan, while Philip supported Conrad de Montferrat. A compromise was eventually reached in which Guy would be king for his lifetime but would be succeeded by Conrad and his heirs. But, the bickering at Acre caused Philip to reach the end of his patience. He left the crusade and returned to France. The three key reasons that prompted Philip's return are summarised in Figure 2.4.

Extend your knowledge

Richard's marriage to Berengaria
Richard's marriage to Berengaria of Navarre was not purely a case of spite against Philip II. A marriage to her would help to secure the south of the Angevin Empire, which bordered on Navarre in northern Spain.

It was important for Richard to marry so that he could produce an heir to secure the future of the Angevin Empire. A male heir would mean that Richard could peacefully pass the empire to his son when he died and his subjects were very keen for him to marry before he risked death by fighting in the crusade. However, although he married Berengaria, they remained childless.

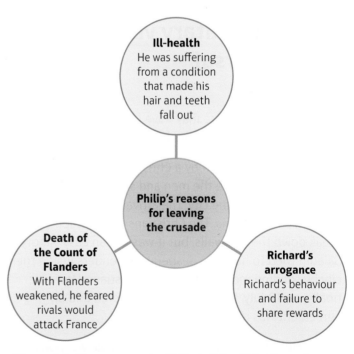

Figure 2.4 The reasons why Philip left the Third Crusade.

Activities

1 Why did Richard and Philip quarrel? Make a list of the reasons.
2 Choose three reasons from your list and develop each reason into an explanation.
3 Study your three reasons. Which is the most important? Discuss your ideas with a partner and record your final judgement. Remember to support your answer with evidence.

The departure of Philip was a serious problem for Richard. Although Philip promised not to attack the Angevin Empire, Richard could not trust him to keep his word. Richard's relationship with the other crusader leaders was no better. He fell out with Leopold of Austria after his men tore down Leopold's flag at Acre, which had been placed in triumph alongside the flags of Richard and Philip. It was claimed that Leopold had no right to display his banner alongside that of kings since Leopold was only a duke. If Leopold displayed his banner, it would also suggest that he had an equal right to a share in the spoils of the Crusade, but both Richard and Philip were determined to keep them for themselves. Leopold, angered by this personal humiliation, left the crusade with a deep hatred for the English king. Richard had lost two important allies.

Richard's military victories at Acre and Arsuf

Acre, July 1191

Richard's victory at Acre may have led to the loss of two allies, but it did demonstrate his skills as a great warrior.

Acre had been besieged by a Christian army since 1189, but they did not have the men and siege equipment needed to capture the city. The arrival of Philip, and then Richard, changed this. The Christians used catapults to break down the city walls, but it was not an easy victory. Saladin tried to help the desperate defenders inside the city by sending men to attack the Christians. However, finally, on 12 July, the Muslims surrendered and an agreement was reached with Saladin:

- The Muslims would hand over their siege weapons and ships, and pay 200,000 gold coins
- Christian prisoners would be released from Saladin's prisons and handed over.
- Saladin would return to the Christians the True Cross*, which he captured at Hattin.

Key term

True Cross*

The name given by Christians for the fragments of wood believed to be from the cross on which Jesus was crucified.

The victory at Acre was of great importance to the Christians. It was a key port and would play a vital role in securing food and military supplies to the crusaders on their journey to Jerusalem. Supplies could be moved more easily by sea than they could by land.

Once the deal was made, the Christians celebrated their entry into the city of Acre. However, it was not long before the agreement broke down:

- Saladin did not release the Christian prisoners.
- He did not hand over the True Cross.
- He gave a note that promised to pay the money instead of the 200,000 gold coins.

Richard believed that Saladin was playing for time and that he was taking the opportunity to build up his strength elsewhere while the crusaders were stuck at Acre with thousands of prisoners. What happened next was an act for which Richard has been condemned by modern historians. On 20 August, with the agreement of his council, he took 2,700 Muslim prisoners from Acre to Saladin's camp. Richard's men beheaded all of them just outside the camp.

Source A

A contemporary image of the siege of Acre.

Opinions about Richard's actions are mixed. The execution of the prisoners has been described as barbarous, and it has also been described as stupid because he could have ransomed them. Baha al-Din, one of Saladin's advisers, suggested that Richard's actions were either driven by revenge for the murder of Christians, or that Richard could not cope with large numbers of prisoners (see Source B).

More recently, some historians have said that the massacre was not unusual for the time, arguing that Richard behaved as a military leader was expected to do (see Interpretation 1). It would have been very difficult for the Christian garrison at Acre to feed the prisoners and there was a chance that they might escape. Indeed, Saladin could be seen as responsible for their deaths because of his delaying tactics. Some have claimed Saladin sacrificed the men to save money.

Source B

Baha al-Din's account of the massacre of the Muslim prisoners at Acre. Baha al-Din was one of Saladin's advisers. He was present at the siege of Acre and wrote an account of the Third Crusade from the Muslim point of view.

It was said that they [the Christians] had killed them in revenge for their men who had been killed or that the king of England had decided to march to Ascalon [another city in the Holy Land] to take control of it and did not think it wise to leave that number [of prisoners] in his rear. God knows best.

Interpretation 1

A modern explanation for Richard's execution of the prisoners from Acre in *Holy Warriors* (2009) by Jonathan Phillips.

Practical strategic reasons were important [in the decision to massacre the Muslim prisoners]. The Christians would not want to guard and feed so many prisoners with the army absent to the south. With every passing day the king could see the chance of victory ebbing away. Saladin's delaying tactics gave the crusaders little choice.

Source C

An image of Richard the Lionheart in mounted combat on crusade in 1191. This 13th-century image of the 'Holy Warrior' is depicted on tiles in Chertsey Abbey in Surrey

The Battle of Arsuf, September 1191

On leaving Acre, Richard marched his troops south towards Jaffa. His expertise as a military leader was shown on this march. The weather was hot, the distance was great and the crusaders were frequently attacked by the Muslims. However, Richard's army marched close to the sea and he organised ships to sail down the coast carrying supplies so that the men could be properly fed and had enough water to drink. The march was so successful that Saladin realised he would have to engage Richard in battle to stop him.

Saladin gathered a huge army on the plain of Arsuf, hoping to end Richard's relentless march. However, in the battle that followed, Richard emerged as the hero. His leadership justified his growing reputation as a great military leader.

Richard carefully set up the formation of his army and ordered them to wait for his signal before they attacked. His intention was to lure in the Muslim army so that he could defeat it in one great charge. However, the constant bombardment of the crusaders by the Muslim horse archers led to a loss of discipline among Richard's troops. Two knights broke ranks and began to chase Saladin's horsemen. They were followed by hundreds of the crusaders. Richard had to act quickly and decisively to restore order. He led a mighty charge into the centre of Saladin's army and forced the Muslims to flee. He was then able to lead his troops into Jaffa, where they began to fortify the city. Richard's victory at Arsuf demonstrated his personal bravery and outstanding leadership skills.

The failure to capture Jerusalem

The first march, October 1191–January 1192

Richard began marching the crusader forces towards Jerusalem. Their progress was slow because of heavy rains. Some of the Christians grew reluctant to advance to the holy city. There were four main reasons for this.

- They feared Saladin's forces would surround them.
- They were worried that they would be cut off from their supplies if they moved too far from the coast.
- Jerusalem was protected by a string of fortresses that were in Muslim hands, and a strong outer wall that would be difficult to break through.
- They believed that even if they did gain control of Jerusalem, they would not be able to hold on to it for long because of a lack of supplies.

As a consequence of these fears, and the difficult conditions they were experiencing, in January 1192 Richard ordered a retreat. The leading crusaders understood why Richard gave this order, but the ordinary soldiers were very disappointed, especially when they considered the hardship they had suffered on the march. Some of the soldiers returned to Acre while Richard marched south to capture Ascalon and repair its defences.

Figure 2.5 A scene from a 14th-century medieval manuscript, the *Luttrell Psalter*. This scene shows Richard the Lionheart fighting Saladin. The two men never actually met in battle. Saladin was not well enough to fight at Arsuf.

The crusaders had not given up. They had come to the Holy Land in order to return Jerusalem to Christian control. There was increasing pressure on Richard to make another attempt to win back Jerusalem quickly.

- He had received news from England of Prince John's rebellion (see page 24), which meant that he needed to return to the Angevin Empire as soon as possible.
- The other important crusader nobles were prepared to march on Jerusalem without Richard and he did not want them to take the glory.

The second march, June–July 1192

The second march began successfully. Within four days they had reached Beit Nuba, which was only 12 miles away from Jerusalem. Furthermore, Saladin was experiencing difficulties in keeping his army together, so there was a good chance that the crusaders could have taken Jerusalem. However, Richard decided that they would not march on the holy city.

- He feared that Saladin would cut his supply lines to the coast if he pushed on.
- It was the height of summer and water was scarce.

- He did not believe that the Christians in the Holy Land could hold the city once the crusading knights returned to Europe.

So, Richard led his army back to the coast.

Exam-style question, Section B

Explain why Richard failed to recapture Jerusalem from Muslim control?

You may use the following in your answer:

- army supplies
- Jerusalem's defences.

You **must** also use information of your own. **12 marks**

Exam tip

This question is about causation. You need to explain rather than describe. Begin by identifying three reasons. Write a couple of sentences to explain how each reason prevented Richard from capturing Jerusalem. To develop your answer with explanation, you could consider the differences between the long-term causes and short-term causes.

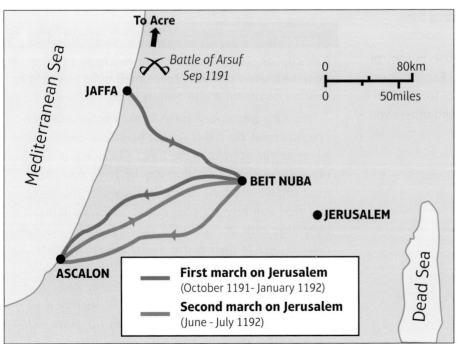

Figure 2.6 A map showing the routes taken by Richard's army in the two marches on Jerusalem, 1191–92.

THINKING HISTORICALLY Cause and Consequence (3a&b)

The might of human agency

1 'Our lack of control'. Work in pairs.

Describe to your partner a situation where things did not work out as you had intended. Then explain how you would have done things differently to make the situation as you would have wanted. Your partner will then tell the group about that situation and whether they think that your alternative actions would have had the desired effect.

2 'The tyranny of failed actions'. Work individually.

Richard the Lionheart and the recapture of Jerusalem

3 a Write down what Richard's aims were.

b Write down what Richard's actions were.

c To what extent were Richard's actions successful in achieving their aims?

d Make a spider diagram: write Richard's actions in the middle and then add as many consequences of his actions as possible around them. Think about the long-term consequences as well as the immediate ones.

e How important were the consequences of Richard's actions for the future of the crusade?

4 To what extent are historical individuals in control of the history they helped to create? Explain your answer in a paragraph, with reference to specific historical examples from this topic and others you have studied.

Victory at Jaffa and the truce, August–September 1192

At the end of July 1192, Saladin launched an attack on Jaffa. Just when it seemed like the city would be lost, Richard arrived and led the attack against Saladin's army. Richard's outstanding fighting skills and the fear he inspired were celebrated in contemporary chronicles (see Source D). After Saladin's first attempt to capture Jaffa was defeated, he swore revenge. On 5 August, he surprised the crusaders with a second effort. However, Richard distinguished himself in battle once more and defeated the attack. The victory owed much to Richard's personal courage (see Source E).

Source D

An account of Richard's actions in driving back Saladin's army on 1 August 1192, from *The Chronicle of the Third Crusade* compiled by a contemporary chronicler, Richard de Templo, in the 1220s.

With no armour on his legs he threw himself into the sea first... and forced his way powerfully on to dry land... The outstanding king shot them [the Muslims] down indiscriminately with a crossbow he was carrying in his hand... At the sight of the king, they had no more spirit in them, they dare not approach him.

Source E

A description of how Richard fought on 5 August 1192 from the *Itinerary of Richard I and Others to the Holy Land* by Geoffrey de Vinsauf, a 13th-century writer.

... the king was a very giant in the battle, and was everywhere in the field, — now here, now there, wherever the attacks of the Turks [Saladin's soldiers] raged the hottest... On that day he performed the most gallant deeds on the furious army of the Turks, and slew numbers with his sword, which shone like lightning; some of them were cloven [cut] in two from their helmet to their teeth, whilst others lost their heads, arms, and other members, which were lopped off at a single blow... Such was his energy amid that host of Turks, that, fearing nothing, he destroyed all around him, mowing men down [with his sword] as reapers mow down the corn with their sickles.

In spite of his success, Richard needed to return home. Saladin was ill and eager to reach a settlement. In September 1192, the two leaders reached the following agreement:

- a three-year truce in the fighting,
- the Christians would control the coastline from Tyre to Jaffa,
- the Muslims would remain in control of Jerusalem,
- Christian pilgrims would have free and safe access to Jerusalem.

Richard did not stay to visit Jerusalem. On 9 October he set sail for home.

Activity

What did Richard achieve on the Third Crusade? Draw one concept map to summarise all his achievements and another to summarise what he failed to achieve.

Summary

- Richard I joined the crusade to free Jerusalem from Muslim control and to achieve glory in war.
- Richard and Philip II of France went on crusade together but quarrels between them led to Philip returning to France in July 1191.
- Richard defeated the Muslims at Acre and Arsuf in 1191. He also massacred 2,700 Muslim prisoners from Acre.
- Richard led two marches on Jerusalem, but fear of being cut off from his supplies meant that he retreated on both occasions before getting to the holy city.
- In September 1192, Richard and Saladin agreed a three-year truce that left the Muslims in control of Jerusalem and gave Christian pilgrims access to the holy places in the city.

Checkpoint

Strengthen

S1 List the factors that led to Richard and Philip quarrelling when they got to Cyprus.

S2 List three difficulties that the crusaders faced on the marches to Jerusalem?

S3 What agreement was reached with the Muslims after the victory at Jaffa?

Challenge

C1 Read the opinions below about Richard's achievements on the crusade. Find evidence to support each opinion and use it to write two paragraphs, one for each statement. Which view has the strongest support? Compare your ideas with a partner and discuss your decision. Write a third paragraph making a judgement on which opinion you agree with and why. Remember to explain your ideas.

Opinion 1: Richard the Lionheart was a great leader and warrior.

Opinion 2: Richard was a failure as a leader of the crusade.

C2 You are a Muslim chronicler. Write an account of Richard's actions during the Third Crusade.

How confident do you feel about your answers to these questions? If you are not sure you answered them well, try discussing what you've written with a partner and note down anything you have missed.

2.3 Aftermath of the crusade

Learning outcomes

- Understand Richard's capture on the way back from the Holy Land.
- Understand the burden of Richard's ransom on England.

Richard was anxious to get back to his empire. While he had been on crusade, his brother John had teamed up with Philip II and attacked Richard's continental lands. Furthermore, his enemies had been giving him a bad name in Europe. The man who Richard humiliated at Acre, Leopold of Austria (see page 50), had spread the rumour that Richard had been behind the murder of Conrad de Montferrat. Conrad, who was Leopold's cousin, had been killed by assassins in 1192.

Richard found that there was virtually no safe route that he could take back home. He headed first for the island of Corfu and then sailed up the Adriatic coast. He could not travel through Italy as he had on his journey to the Holy Land because it was now full of his enemies.

Richard's capture and the demands for ransom

In November, Richard was shipwrecked off the northern Adriatic coast and he and his companions were forced to travel across land. They disguised themselves as pilgrims, but it was not long before he was recognised. Richard was arrested and imprisoned by Leopold of Austria. In February 1193, Leopold sold Richard to Henry VI, the Holy Roman Emperor. The emperor was overjoyed with his prisoner. He wrote gleefully to Philip II to give him the news of Richard's captivity.

Richard's life was not at risk. In the chivalric code, the purpose of capturing a great knight was to claim a ransom, and Richard would be worth a very high price. Soon Henry, Leopold and Philip were haggling about the sum they should demand. Eventually they agreed that they would demand the huge sum of 100,000 marks (about £66,000) plus an additional 50,000 marks, which was to be covered by sending over other noble hostages. The ransom money would be split between Henry and Leopold. Philip would not receive any money, but he was mostly concerned that the ransom would not be set too low so that Richard would be released quickly.

The burden of the ransom

The ransom was a very heavy demand to make on England. The population had already paid a high price to equip Richard's crusade. John had no desire to pay the ransom. He had spread the rumour that Richard was dead before travelling to France to do homage to Philip in the hope of securing the Angevin continental lands for himself. Finally, he claimed that he was the legitimate king as he was Richard's true heir. However, at this point, the letter from Henry, containing news of Richard's captivity and the demand for the ransom, arrived in England. It was ordered that the oaths of fealty to Richard must be honoured and that his ransom paid. Envoys* were sent to visit Richard in captivity and negotiate his release.

Key term

Envoy*
A messenger sent by one government to talk with another government.

Richard was found in good spirits. He sneered at the idea that John could steal his throne, claiming that, 'My brother John is not a man to conquer a country if there is anyone to offer even the feeblest resistance'. Although Henry put Richard on trial, in front of an assembly of loyal German princes, for betraying the Holy Land, Richard put up such an impressive defence that he swayed a number of the princes to his side. As a result, the emperor dropped the charges and Richard agreed to the ransom if the emperor would act as the peacemaker between Richard and Philip once he was released. Richard then sent the envoys back to England to collect the ransom and began preparing for his release.

Richard's preparations for his swift return to England were too optimistic. The sum of 100,000 marks was an enormous demand to make. In modern money this sum was worth as much as £2 billion (see Interpretation 1) and it could not easily be collected, especially after all the money that had been paid to fund the crusade.

Interpretation 1

Historian Frank McLynn explains the difficulty of paying Richard's ransom in *Lionheart and Lackland: King Richard, King John and the Wars of Conquest* (2006).

The scale of [the] task should not be underestimated. 100,000 marks or £66,000 – maybe £2 billion in today's money – was an enormous sum for any medieval state to raise, as may be seen from everyday comparisons. At the time a sheep cost one penny, a pig sixpence… and soldiers were paid twopence a day; the ransom was three times the annual expenditure of the English government. Moreover, this extra sum had to be found in a society that had already been mulcted [taxed] by the Saladin Tithe and drained by other taxes to pay for the Third Crusade.

It is little surprise that, very soon, both Richard and his mother, Eleanor, were despairing about whether he should ever be set free. Eleanor wrote a letter to the pope pleading for his intervention to save her son, while Richard, in his captivity, composed a song lamenting his long imprisonment (see Source A).

Source A

Part of a song written by Richard in 1193 while he was being held captive by the Holy Roman Emperor, Henry VI.

I have many friends, but poor are their gifts;
Shame on them, if for my ransom
I must be two winters imprisoned…
I don't say this for their reproach,
But still I am imprisoned.

John, on the other hand, did not despair. In a secret letter in January 1194, he and Philip II offered the emperor 80,000 marks not to release Richard until at least the autumn.

Eleanor took charge of collecting the ransom to pay for Richard's freedom. Figure 2.7 shows how Richard's ransom was paid:

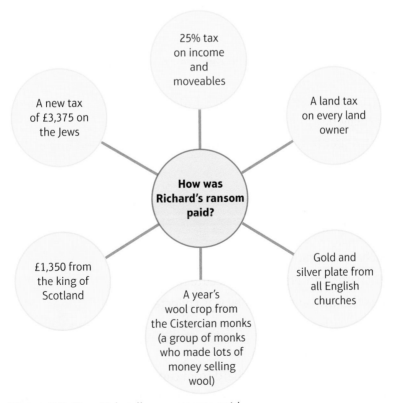

Figure 2.7 How Richard's ransom was paid.

The fact that Eleanor managed to gather in this huge amount of money shows the wealth of England at this time. Nevertheless, it took six months to collect. England's finances had not recovered by the time John came to the throne five years later. He found himself short of money compared to Richard, but his demands for taxes caused great resentment because the people had already paid so much.

Activity ?

Write a letter from Eleanor to the pope requesting help to get Richard released from captivity. Before you start, make a list of the points she would make about Richard to encourage the pope to help. Use these points to help you write a convincing argument.

Richard's return to England

Richard was released from captivity on 4 February 1194. He had been in captivity for one year and six weeks. The ransom was not the only price paid; in a secret agreement with the emperor, Richard agreed to hand over the English crown to Henry VI and to receive it back from him as a vassal. Richard set off immediately for England.

Richard landed at Sandwich on the Kent coast in March. His return was greeted with great celebrations, but his stay in England was not to last long. He crushed what was left of John's revolt, laying siege to the castles of Tickhill and Nottingham, and confiscating lands that had been held by his brother. Finally, he appointed Hubert Walter, who had recently been made the Archbishop of Canterbury, as the head of his government in England. In May, Richard departed for the continent to restore his control over the Angevin territory. He was never to return to England.

Summary

- Richard was captured on his way home from the Holy Land by Leopold of Austria.
- Prince John spread the rumour that Richard was dead and joined with Philip II to attack Richard's Angevin continental lands.
- Richard was sold to Henry VI, the Holy Roman Emperor, who demanded a ransom of 100,000 marks.
- Eleanor of Aquitaine oversaw the collection of the ransom; the huge sum demanded placed an enormous burden on England's finances.
- Richard was released from captivity after being held for more than a year; he returned to England where he swiftly put down John's rebellion.
- Richard appointed Hubert Walter to take charge of the government and left England in May 1194; he would never again return to England.

Checkpoint

Strengthen

S1 Give one reason why Richard was captured.

S2 Give two reasons why Richard's captors did not execute him.

S3 List three sources from which the ransom money was collected.

Challenge

C1 Why did Prince John claim Richard was dead?

C2 Why did it take more than a year to release Richard from captivity?

How confident do you feel about your answers to these questions? If you are not sure you answered them well, try plotting the key points on a concept map and then use that to help you write your answers.

The competing aims of Richard, John and Philip II in Normandy

From 1194–1204, Richard, John and Philip II devoted their energies to trying to win control of Normandy. Ultimately, Philip wanted control over the whole of France. This inevitably brought him into conflict with Richard and, later, John.

When Richard returned to Normandy in 1194, it was weak as a result of John's treachery and Philip's attacks.

- Philip had persuaded a number of barons who held castles on the border between France and Normandy to switch their allegiance to France. As a consequence, Philip had been able to invade Normandy more easily.
- Philip and John had conquered much of western Normandy including two important harbours. This, together with an alliance with the Count of Flanders, meant that Philip could now threaten the Angevins by sea as well as by land.
- Philip took control of the strategically important Vexin. John did not stop him.
- The greatest gain by Philip was the great castle at Gisors. It was vital to the defences of Normandy because it was positioned between the French capital at Paris and the Norman capital of Rouen.

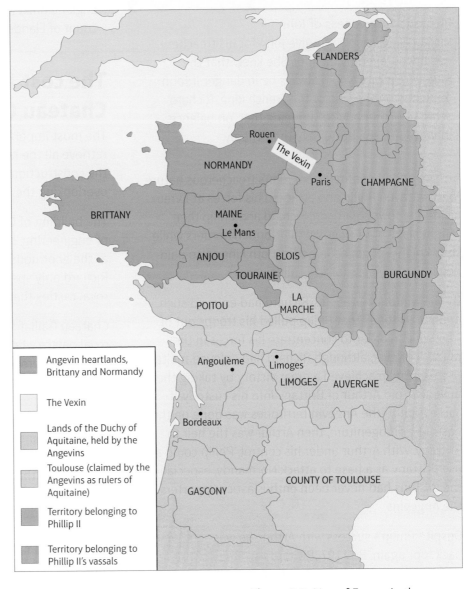

Figure 2.8 Map of France in the reigns of Richard and John. Although the Angevins controlled large parts of France, the French king was the feudal overlord of the whole country.

Map legend:

- Angevin heartlands, Brittany and Normandy
- The Vexin
- Lands of the Duchy of Aquitaine, held by the Angevins
- Toulouse (claimed by the Angevins as rulers of Aquitaine)
- Territory belonging to Phillip II
- Territory belonging to Phillip II's vassals

The problem of John was easily settled by Richard. John knew that he was no match for his elder brother. He met Richard at his court in Normandy and threw himself upon Richard's mercy. It would have been understandable if Richard had considered John to be his lifelong enemy and ordered his punishment. However, Richard forgave him, blaming Philip for misleading his brother (see page 24). With John now on his side, Richard had only one enemy to attack.

(see page 24)

Extend your knowledge

Richard's forgiveness of John

Richard's decision to forgive John for his treachery was encouraged by Eleanor. She knew that the Angevin Empire would always be in danger if John remained on the side of the French king. Richard acted upon her advice, agreeing that, on balance, John would be a better ally than enemy.

Richard soon benefited from John's treacherous nature. John betrayed Philip and attacked his forces at Evreux, killing the town's garrison. Richard and Philip then fought siege after siege on the Norman borders while their knights engaged in battle. Both kings also paid neighbouring lords for their allegiance.

By the winter of 1195–96, Richard had enjoyed such a run of victories that Philip pulled his troops out of Aquitaine in order to concentrate his forces in the north. However, although Richard had enjoyed military success, Philip achieved a great victory by taking the nine-year-old Arthur of Brittany into his custody. If succession to the Angevin territories was done on the basis of primogeniture, then Arthur was the heir to Brittany. With Arthur under his control, Philip could also use Brittany as a base to attack Normandy, especially as the Bretons had never been enthusiastic supporters of the Angevins.

Despite Philip's success with Arthur, he was soon on the back foot again. By 1197, Richard's strategy of bribing the vassals on Philip's borders to switch allegiance was working. Philip found that he was surrounded by hostile neighbours. Richard also used a trade embargo* to persuade the Count of Flanders to support the Angevin Empire. In addition, Arthur had returned to Brittany and Philip's influence over the Bretons was reduced.

Key term

Trade embargo*

A restriction on trade for political purposes. The suspension of the valuable wool trade between England and Flanders was enough to encourage the Count of Flanders to support Richard instead of Philip.

The cost and importance of Chateau Gaillard

The most important element in Richard's strategy to retrieve all the lands taken by Philip in his absence was the construction of a great castle on the River Seine overlooking the Vexin. This castle was Chateau Gaillard.

The building of Chateau Gaillard was a magnificent feat of engineering. It was built in just two years (1196–98) at the enormous cost of £12,000. This was a vast sum: Richard only spent £7,000 on the construction of all the royal castles that he built in England during his reign.

Chateau Gaillard was both a defensive structure and a royal palace where Richard could hold court. Its defences were considered to be the finest in Europe. By this time, most warfare focused on besieging castles rather than pitched battles on an open field. Besiegers concentrated on using catapults to launch stones at the weak points in the walls and engineers to tunnel under the walls to cause them to collapse. A key strength of Chateau Gaillard was that it was built hundreds of feet above the town and harbour at Les Andelys, which made it difficult to tunnel under its walls. Even more importantly, it had round walls. Catapults were successful in a siege when the stones struck the angles on castle walls as these were the weakest points. With no angles, Chateau Gaillard seemed impossible to attack.

Source A

The ruins of Chateau Gaillard as it stands today. The strong defences shown in the round walls of the tower, which loom over the river, are clearly visible.

Historians used to assume that Chateau Gaillard was built for defensive purposes, situated as it was on the border of Philip's lands. More recently, some historians have claimed that it was part of an aggressive strategy; it would be the base for Richard to launch a campaign to recapture the Vexin. The castle was on a direct route from Rouen, the capital of Normandy, from which supplies could be transported to the troops at Chateau Gaillard. Chateau Gaillard could then be used as a base to launch attacks on nearby French castles, such as the one at Gisors. This meant the castle was very important to Richard's plans for restoring his empire and the events following its construction support this theory. In September 1198, Richard launched a surprise attack on Philip's army, which was forced to retreat to Gisors. Richard captured over 90 knights and 200 horses, but he did not have the siege engines to attack the castle at Gisors. Nevertheless, by the following January, Richard almost controlled the Vexin, and he and Philip negotiated a truce.

The death of Richard the Lionheart

The negotiations for a truce were still going on when, in late March 1199, Richard decided to survey the defences of his troops besieging a small castle near the city of Limoges. Without wearing his armour, he strolled along his line of defence. From the castle a single archer armed with a crossbow shot a bolt at Richard, which hit him in the shoulder. Although the wound was not fatal, Richard broke off the arrow shaft and left the bolt in his shoulder. Surgeons removed the bolt, but the wound became infected. Within a week, infection had spread and, on 6 April 1199, Richard died.

Activity ?

You and your partner are 12th-century chroniclers. One of you is English, the other is French. Write an account of Richard's campaigns from his release from captivity in 1194 to his death in 1199. Compare your accounts. What are the similarities and differences?

John and the loss of Normandy

The catalyst for war – the marriage to Isabelle of Angouleme

When John became king in 1199, he inherited an empire that was almost as complete as that which Richard had taken over a decade earlier. Five years later, John had lost Normandy to Philip. The collapse of Angevin power on the continent began with John's marriage to Isabelle of Angouleme. It provided the excuse for Philip to launch an attack that ultimately left him in possession of Normandy.

Isabelle was the heiress to Angouleme, an area of land between Poitou and Gascony. Possession of this land would help John to control the area more effectively. The problem was that Isabelle of Angouleme was already betrothed* to John's vassal, Hugh de Lusignan.

Key term

Betrothed*
A binding promise to marry.

John ignored the rights of his vassal and married Isabelle. He would probably have been safe if he had offered lands to Hugh in compensation for his loss. However, John acted recklessly. When Hugh complained, John suggested that they both choose champions to fight for them and the winner would take Isabelle. Since John's champion would undoubtedly have been William Marshal, who was regarded as the greatest knight of the age, Hugh was not prepared to agree to such a scheme. Instead he turned to John's feudal overlord, Philip II, and appealed for justice.

Source B

A 13th-century French wall painting showing Eleanor of Aquitaine and Isabelle of Angouleme riding through France.

Stage 1	King John's marriage to Isabelle of Angouleme causes Hugh de Lusignan to appeal for justice to Philip II of France.
Stage 2	John's refusal to attend Philip's court in 1202 gives Philip the right to declare Normandy forfeit and to launch an attack on John.
Stage 3	Arthur of Brittany pays homage to Philip for the Angevin territories in France.
Stage 4	Arthur is murdered while being held prisoner by John. Many of John's barons defect, and lords from Maine, Anjou and Poitou pay homage to Philip. The Bretons also put their support behind the French king.
Stage 5	Philip takes possession of Normandy after his successful seige at Chateau Gaillard. John is too slow to respond to the seige.

Figure 2.9 Stages in the loss of Normandy, 1200–1204.

John had acknowledged Philip as his overlord in a treaty in 1200 (see page 20). This meant that Philip had the feudal right to launch an attack on John as he was being a disobedient vassal. He summoned John to his court in Paris at Easter 1202 to answer charges. John refused to attend. He claimed that, as Duke of Normandy, he was not obliged to travel beyond the border of his duchy. However, the complicated number of different titles and feudal obligations came into play here. Philip argued that John had been summoned not as Duke of Normandy but as Count of Poitou, and was obliged to attend Philip's court.

John's refusal to go to Paris allowed Philip to declare all John's lands forfeit and accept Arthur's homage for the Angevin territories. In the eyes of the French king, Arthur was now the lord of the Angevin lands in France, except Normandy, which Philip claimed for himself.

The problems John faced

The difficulty of John's task in defending Normandy was clear from the start (see Figure 2.10 on page 63). However, John was an able military leader and skilled in the besieging of castles. In the summer of 1202, he led a spectacular march to Mirebeau where Arthur was besieging the castle. John covered the 80 miles from Le Mans to Mirebeau in just 48 hours. He took Arthur by surprise, captured him and relieved the siege. At this point, there appeared to be every chance that John could succeed in holding Normandy. However, John lost this advantage.

- At Easter in 1203, John had Arthur murdered (see page 21).
- News of Arthur's murder led to the defection of many of John's barons to Philip; this included large numbers of Norman barons. Lords from Maine, Anjou and Poitou also did homage to Philip.
- The Bretons, no longer needing to be loyal to John in order to keep Arthur safe, gave their support to Philip.

Problem 1: The English barons	**Problem 2: Expensive allies**
The English barons did not want another war: the crusade, Richard's ransom and Richard's wars in France had cost them a lot of money.	John had to give money to the allies that Richard had made on the continent in order to keep their support. This was very expensive.
Problem 3: Poitou	**Problem 4: Arthur**
Poitou had a long history of resisting Angevin control which meant that John could not concentrate his forces in Normandy.	Arthur was under the control of Philip and, after doing homage for the Angevin territories, he led an army southwards to attack John's castles in Poitou whilst Philip attacked Normandy.

Figure 2.10 Problems that John faced with Normandy.

The loss of Normandy, 1204

John's act of homage to Philip in 1200 undermined his position with the Norman barons. When they began to defect to Philip after the murder of Arthur, they could justify their behaviour by claiming that they were submitting to their ultimate feudal lord (Philip) because their immediate overlord (John) had broken feudal law.

John's decision to return to England in the autumn of 1203 was also unwise. It appeared to the Normans that he had deserted them. William Marshal criticised John and argued that he was to blame for the problems that he now faced (see Source C). Some historians also argue that John struggled in the war against Philip because he did not have enough money to pay for it. Richard's crusade, ransom and constant warfare meant John had little money, whilst Philip had reformed his finances and now had much more money than John.

Everybody expected John to make a speedy return to Normandy, but he did not. While he was in England, John secured funding for a campaign in Normandy with the agreement that the barons would pay a scutage (see page 28). In the meantime, he was relying on the pope to help secure a peace treaty between himself and Philip. However, Philip had no interest in peace and John was mistaken in his belief that he still had plenty of time to prepare for a new campaign in France.

Source C

William Marshal's criticism of John's action in the winter of 1203. These words were recorded in *The History of William Marshal*, which was written shortly after his death in 1219.

Sire... you have few friends, if you choose to strengthen your enemies, then your own power will decline; if a man strengthens his enemies, it is justifiable for men to attack him... You paid no attention to the first sign of discontent, but it would have been better for all of us if you had.

On 6 March 1204, Chateau Gaillard fell to Philip. He had been besieging the castle since the summer of 1203. The inhabitants of the castle had been expecting John to send relief to help them withstand Philip's siege, but that relief never came. Even a castle like Chateau Gaillard could not withstand a long siege without outside help.

Once Chateau Gaillard had fallen, Philip was able to overrun Normandy. Town after town fell to him. On 24 June 1204, the capital city of Rouen surrendered to Philip. He was now lord of Normandy. John's inability to defend the duchy meant that he was criticised by his subjects as a 'softsword' who had failed as a warrior-king. He spent the next decade struggling to get Normandy back.

THINKING HISTORICALLY — Cause and Consequence (4a&b)

Fragile history

Nothing that happens is inevitable. Sometimes things happen due to the actions of an individual or chance events that no one anticipated. Something could have altered or someone could have chosen differently, bringing about a very different outcome. What actually occurred in the past did happen, but it did not have to be like that.

Work on your own and answer the questions below. When you have answered the questions, discuss the answers in a group. Then have a class vote.

Perceived reasons for King John's loss of Normandy

The ambitions of the French king	King John's marriage to Isabelle of Angouleme	The murder of Arthur of Brittany	King John's skills as a warrior	The defection of King John's barons	The fall of Chateau Gaillard in 1204	The state of England's finances in John's reign

1   Consider King John's loss of Normandy.
  a   How did the ambitions of the French king affect the loss of Normandy?
  b   Had King John been a more obedient vassal, would the ambitions of the French king be relevant?

2   Consider John's motivations.
  a   What might have happened had John not murdered Arthur of Brittany? Would all the other causes still be relevant?
  b   What might have happened had John put Arthur on trial?
  c   How did the defection of John's barons affect the outcome?

3   Write down any events that you think could be called 'chance events'. How important were these in causing the loss of Normandy?

4   Imagine you were alive in 1199, when John became king. Write a paragraph explaining how you think the control of the Angevin Empire might change in the next 16 years. Remember not to use the benefit of hindsight!

5   Have a class vote: was the loss of Normandy inevitable? Be prepared to back up your decision.

Summary

- Richard built Chateau Gaillard at great expense. It threatened Philip's control of the Vexin.
- John's marriage to Isabelle of Angouleme provided Philip with the justification to attack the Angevin Empire.
- John lost the support of many of his barons after the murder of Arthur.
- Philip captured Chateau Gaillard in March 1204; by summer Philip had control of Normandy.

Checkpoint

Strengthen

S1   Write a paragraph describing Chateau Gaillard.
S2   Who was Isabelle of Angouleme and why was she important?

Challenge

C1   What was the consequence of the murder of Arthur on John's campaign in Normandy?

How confident do you feel about your answers to these questions? If you are not sure you answered them well, try the activities on page 65.

Recap: Involvement overseas, 1189–1204

Recall quiz

1 What was a crusade?
2 List three reasons why men joined the Third Crusade.
3 Who was Saladin?
4 List three reasons why Richard quarrelled with Philip II during the crusade.
5 What agreement did Richard make with Saladin in September 1192?
6 Who captured Richard on his return from the crusade?
7 How much was Richard's ransom?
8 Give one reason why Chateau Gaillard was difficult to attack.
9 Give one consequence of John's marriage to Isabelle of Angouleme.
10 What was the significance of Philip's capture of Chateau Gaillard in March 1204?

Activities

1 Study Source C on page 63. Using your knowledge, make a list of the ways in which John's actions helped to strengthen his enemies.
2 Imagine you are one of John's Norman barons. Write a paragraph to explain your decision to switch to Philip's side.
3 Compare Richard and John's efforts to keep control of Normandy. Draw up a table with two columns, one for Richard and one for John, and write down the actions each king took in Normandy.
4 Using the table you created for question 2, discuss with a partner the question: 'Why did Richard succeed and John fail?' Write a paragraph answering the question.
5 In small groups, discuss the statement: Philip's cunning, rather than John's mistakes, was the main reason for the loss of Normandy in 1204. Do you agree with this assessment? Were there other factors involved? Write down your ideas.

Exam-style question, Section B

'King John's marriage to Isabelle of Angouleme is the main reason why he lost Normandy in the summer of 1204'.

How far do you agree? Explain your answer.

You may use the following in your answer:

• King Philip of France
• Chateau Gaillard.

You **must** also use information of your own. **16 marks**

Exam tip

When answering questions on why things happen, good answers will clearly link the identified reasons to the outcome. Write an explanation for each of these factors, and at least one additional factor, and link the reason to the loss of Normandy in 1204.

Writing historically: building sentences

Successful historical writing uses a range of sentence structures to achieve clarity, precision and emphasis.

Learning outcomes

By the end of this lesson, you will understand how to:

- use and position subordinate clauses to link ideas with clarity and precision
- manipulate sentence structure to emphasise key ideas.

Definitions

Clause: a group of words or unit of meaning that contains a verb and can form part or all of a sentence.

Single clause sentence: a sentence containing just one clause.

Subordinating conjunction: a word used to link a dependent clause to the main clause of a sentence.

Compare the two drafts of sentences below, written in response to this exam-style question:

> Explain why men joined the Third Crusade. **(12 marks)**

These points are written in pairs of unlinked, **single clause sentences**.

> Men went to fight when they were promised a full indulgence. This meant they would go straight to heaven when they died.
>
> Killing was a sin. The crusade was seen as a 'just war' and so the Church approved.
>
> Baldwin toured Wales encouraging recruitment. He enlisted 3,000 crusaders.

The relationship between these points is made clear with subordinating conjunctions.

> Men went to fight when they were promised a full indulgence because this meant they would go straight to heaven when they died.
>
> Although killing was a sin, the crusade was seen as a 'just' war and so the Church approved.
>
> After Baldwin toured Wales, he enlisted 3,000 crusaders.

1. Which responses are more clearly expressed? Write a sentence or two explaining your answer.

Subordinating conjunctions can link ideas to indicate:

- an explanation: e.g. 'because', 'as', 'in order that', etc
- a condition: e.g. 'if', 'unless', etc
- a comparison: e.g. 'although', 'whereas', etc
- a sequence: 'when', 'as', 'before', 'until', etc.

2. How many different ways can you use subordinating conjunctions to link these pairs of ideas, clearly expressing the relationship between them?

> Primogeniture meant eldest sons inherited everything. Younger sons hoped to win lands abroad.

> Feudal lords joined to prove their worth. Their knights joined as part of knight service.

How can I structure my sentences for clarity and emphasis?

In sentences where ideas are linked with subordinate conjunctions, there is:

- a main clause that gives the central point of the sentence
- a dependent, subordinate clause that adds more information about that central point.

Different sentence structures can alter the emphasis of your writing. Look at these sentences that have been used to introduce responses to the exam-style question on the previous page.

Compare these two versions of the first sentence:

> Although killing was a sin, the crusade was seen as a 'just war' and so the Church approved.
> The pope offered a full indulgence to the crusaders.

> The crusade was seen as a 'just war' and so the Church approved although killing was a sin.
> The pope offered a full indulgence to the crusaders.

This is the main clause in this sentence

This is a subordinate clause. It is linked to the main clause with a subordinating conjunction.

3a. Which clause is given more emphasis in each version? Why?

b. Which version do you prefer? Write a sentence or two explaining your decision.

The second sentence in the response above is much shorter than the first sentence:

4. In both responses, the second sentence is much shorter than the first sentence. Why do you think the writer chose to give this point additional emphasis by structuring it as a short sentence? Write a sentence or two explaining your ideas.

5a. Experiment with different ways of sequencing the three pieces of information in the response above, linking all, some, or none of them with subordinating conjunctions:

- Killing was a sin
- The crusade was seen as a 'just war' and so the Church approved
- The pope offered a full indulgence to the crusaders.

b. Which version do you prefer? One of yours, or the original version? Write a sentence or two explaining your decision.

Improving an answer

6. Now look at the notes below written in response to the exam-style question on the previous page.

> The pope called on Christians to defend the Holy Land.   Archbishop Baldwin recruited volunteers.
> The pope offered a full indulgence.   He encouraged men to 'take the cross'.
> This guaranteed entry into heaven.   He enlisted 3,000 crusaders.

a. Experiment with different ways of sequencing and structuring all the information in sentences. Try to write at least three different versions.

b. Which version do you prefer? Write a sentence or two explaining your decision.

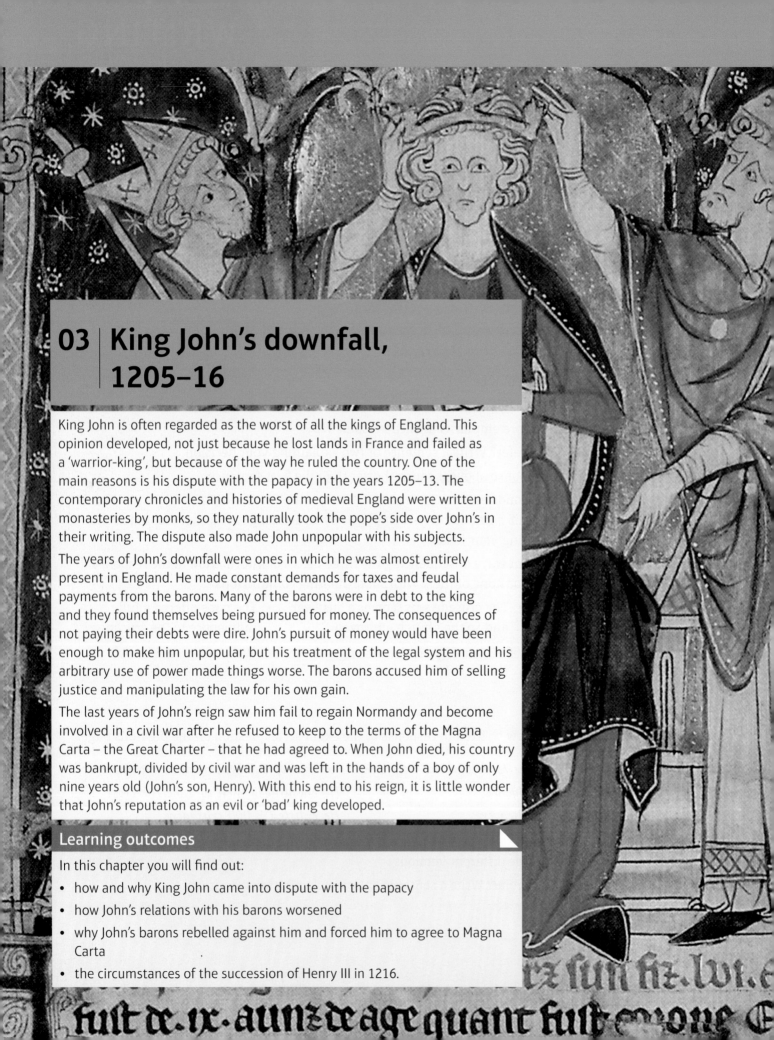

03 | King John's downfall, 1205–16

King John is often regarded as the worst of all the kings of England. This opinion developed, not just because he lost lands in France and failed as a 'warrior-king', but because of the way he ruled the country. One of the main reasons is his dispute with the papacy in the years 1205–13. The contemporary chronicles and histories of medieval England were written in monasteries by monks, so they naturally took the pope's side over John's in their writing. The dispute also made John unpopular with his subjects.

The years of John's downfall were ones in which he was almost entirely present in England. He made constant demands for taxes and feudal payments from the barons. Many of the barons were in debt to the king and they found themselves being pursued for money. The consequences of not paying their debts were dire. John's pursuit of money would have been enough to make him unpopular, but his treatment of the legal system and his arbitrary use of power made things worse. The barons accused him of selling justice and manipulating the law for his own gain.

The last years of John's reign saw him fail to regain Normandy and become involved in a civil war after he refused to keep to the terms of the Magna Carta – the Great Charter – that he had agreed to. When John died, his country was bankrupt, divided by civil war and was left in the hands of a boy of only nine years old (John's son, Henry). With this end to his reign, it is little wonder that John's reputation as an evil or 'bad' king developed.

Learning outcomes

In this chapter you will find out:

- how and why King John came into dispute with the papacy
- how John's relations with his barons worsened
- why John's barons rebelled against him and forced him to agree to Magna Carta
- the circumstances of the succession of Henry III in 1216.

3.1 The dispute with the papacy

King John's reputation has been badly affected by his dispute with the papacy in the years 1205–13. At this time, history was recorded by monks, and it is not surprising that they were highly critical of a king who came into conflict with the Church. Their accounts of John's wickedness are clearly exaggerated. Historical records show him acting in exactly the way a medieval person was expected to behave towards the Church.

However, John's dispute with the papacy had a significant impact on his reign; it undermined his authority over his subjects and even threatened the possibility of an invasion by the French king, justified as a crusade.

The causes of the dispute

At the heart of the dispute was a clash of personalities. John wished to control the Church and force it to accept his demands. However, John was unlucky that he was up against one of the most energetic and forceful popes of the Middle Ages, Pope Innocent III. Innocent was determined to force kings to recognise that they were the vassals of the papacy.

The dispute began in July 1205, when Hubert Walter, the Archbishop of Canterbury, died. Walter was one of Richard's old counsellors. John saw the opportunity to appoint to a new archbishop of his own choice. This was particularly important because the Archbishop of Canterbury had a leading role in John's government as an adviser.

The archbishop was elected by the monks of Canterbury, but John assumed that he would be able to persuade them to choose his candidate. This was not unreasonable – his father and brother had chosen their archbishops. However, the monks chose their own candidate, a Canterbury monk named Reginald, instead of John's candidate, John de Gray (the bishop of Norwich). Both sides appealed to the pope. However, instead of choosing between the two candidates, Innocent III chose his own, Stephen Langton.

John was furious when he heard the news. He claimed that Langton was unknown to him and had been in the service of his enemy, France, (Langton had been teaching in Paris). He also claimed that Innocent was ignoring the principle that the king of England had a right to appoint his own archbishops. In spite of John's opposition, Innocent did not back down and he made Langton archbishop.

Source A

Pope Innocent III shown in a 13th-century Italian wall painting.

Extend your knowledge

Pope Innocent III
Innocent III was elected as pope in 1198. He was an exceptionally young pope at 37 years old, whereas his immediate predecessors had all been old men. He was an energetic pope and was determined to assert the authority of the papacy over the European kings. He claimed the right to judge all men, whilst none but God could judge him.

Figure 3.1 The conflicting arguments of King John and Pope Innocent III.

John immediately reacted by punishing those he considered to be guilty of undermining his rights to choose his archbishop.

- He refused to allow Stephen Langton into the kingdom.
- He expelled the Canterbury monks from their monastery.
- He seized the land held by Italian clergy in England. This was intended to punish the Italian-born pope for his interference in the English Church.

John may have believed his actions would put pressure on the pope to agree that the king of England could choose his own archbishop, but Innocent was just as stubborn as John. He also had powerful weapons that he could use to force John into submission: Interdict and excommunication (see page 14).

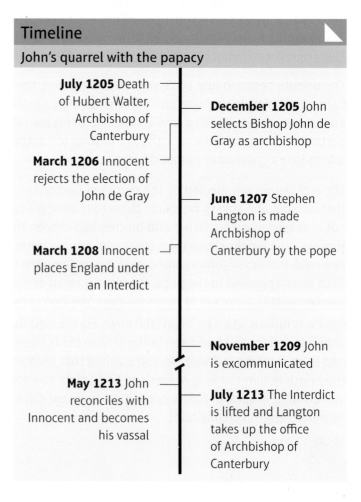

Timeline

John's quarrel with the papacy

July 1205 Death of Hubert Walter, Archbishop of Canterbury

December 1205 John selects Bishop John de Gray as archbishop

March 1206 Innocent rejects the election of John de Gray

June 1207 Stephen Langton is made Archbishop of Canterbury by the pope

March 1208 Innocent places England under an Interdict

November 1209 John is excommunicated

May 1213 John reconciles with Innocent and becomes his vassal

July 1213 The Interdict is lifted and Langton takes up the office of Archbishop of Canterbury

The Interdict and its impact on everyday life

Innocent sent three bishops to England to persuade John to accept Stephen Langton, but John would not give in. In March 1208, Innocent responded by placing England under a sentence of Interdict. This was a very serious punishment. It meant that the people of England were denied access to the Christian sacraments* that were an essential part of their faith.

The consequences of the Interdict on people in England are summarised in Figure 3.2.

Key term

Sacrament*

An important Christian rite or ceremony. There are seven sacraments in the Catholic Church, including baptism, marriage, and anointing the sick with holy oil.

Figure 3.2 The consequences of the Interdict.

John reacted by punishing those whom he blamed for the Interdict; the clergymen who supported the pope. John took the opportunity to enrich himself at their expense by seizing the revenue for their confiscated properties, and he also took a stand against the bad behaviour of some monks by arresting their mistresses (see Interpretation 1).

Source B

The terrible impact that an Interdict had on a king's subjects was described by Abbot Ralph of Coggeshall in 1200. Ralph was talking about a similar Interdict in France – he destroyed the records of the Interdict in England after John's reconciliation with the papacy.

O what a horrible and miserable spectacle it was to see in every city the sealed doors of the churches, Christians shut out from entry as though they were dogs, the cessation of divine office [the prayers sung every day by the monks], the withholding of the sacrament of the body and blood of our Lord [Holy Communion]... the bodies of the dead not given to burial according to Christian rites, of whom the stink infected the air and the horrible sight filled with horror the minds of the living.

Interpretation 1

Historian Ralph Turner, in his biography, *King John, England's Evil King?* (2005), gives his interpretation of John's reaction to the Interdict.

[King John] ordered the arrest of all priests' and clerks' mistresses, whom they had persisted in keeping despite the Church's repeated legislation mandating [requiring] celibacy*. Because the clerics were allowed to purchase their lovers' release, the king also gained revenue.

Royal reprisals mainly took the form of confiscation of clerical property... He commanded that royal custodians take into their hand 'all the lands and goods of abbots, priors, and all religious, and the clergy of [those dioceses] who do not wish to celebrate divine services'. John's confiscation of ecclesiastical [Church] wealth improved his financial position... Yet his subjects could quickly grasp the reasoning behind such an act, since they were familiar with the feudal concept of confiscation for default of service.

* Celibacy: being unmarried or not involved in sexual relationships

The Interdict allowed John to acquire a new source of revenue that he badly needed. This extra revenue meant John had little incentive to reach an agreement with the pope. However, John did want religious life in his kingdom to continue as normally as possible. He did not want to drive his subjects into opposition, and indeed most of them supported him. Only three of his bishops left for the continent and there was no rebellion in England. John even benefited from his bishops exiling themselves as he could claim the income from vacant bishoprics*. This was also true of vacant abbacies*.

Churches coped with the Interdict by holding services outside their doors and, by 1209, Innocent had given permission for churches to hold services behind closed doors and to give Holy Communion to the dying. This has led some historians to claim that the Interdict was a hardship, but nothing more.

Key terms

Bishopric*

The diocese of a bishop – in other words, the area of the country the bishop was responsible for both spiritually and as a feudal tenant-in-chief. If a bishopric was vacant, this meant that there was no bishop overseeing the diocese – either because one had not yet been appointed or because the bishop was in exile. The king could claim the revenues and taxes from the bishopric until a bishop was appointed or returned from exile.

Abbacy*

The area of land that an abbot was responsible for both spiritually and as a feudal lord.

The excommunication of King John

The Interdict did not have the impact that Innocent had expected. Therefore, Innocent needed to use his last and most dangerous weapon: excommunication.

On 8 November 1209, John was excommunicated. His excommunication meant that all Christians, including his barons, were no longer obliged to obey him. More of John's bishops now left England while his barons became increasingly discontented. Although the Church

encouraged barons to turn away from John, it was not an easy choice for them to make. John could confiscate their lands and property if they did not do their full feudal service to him. So, obeying the Church could ruin them and their families. In the end, the majority of barons chose to continue their allegiance to the king, but they resented John for placing them in such a difficult position.

Activities ?

1   Write a letter as Innocent III to King John in 1208, explaining why he should obey 'your' orders and the consequences of disobeying them.

2   Swap your letter with a partner. Have you included the same points? Note down any differences.

3   Write King John's reply to your partner's letter.

The significance of the reconciliation

At first, John's excommunication did not have the desired effect either. John still did not submit to Innocent and grew richer as he was claiming the income from seven bishoprics and 17 abbacies. In fact, it is estimated that John gained £13,500 a year from confiscated Church property and vacant bishoprics. However, as his enemies on the continent gathered against him, John was finally forced to seek a settlement with the papacy. By 1213, England was threatened with an invasion by Prince Louis of France (Philip II's eldest son) and this invasion would have the blessing of the pope as a holy crusade if John did not submit to him.

In early 1213, John sent envoys to Innocent to agree terms. Innocent agreed to lift the Interdict and excommunication if John submitted to the following terms:

- Stephen Langton would be allowed to come to England as Archbishop of Canterbury.
- All the churchmen who had fled England during the quarrel were to be returned to their offices and their property was to be restored.
- John was to pay £8,000 as an immediate compensation to the pope, and £27,000 in total.
- If John broke the agreement, he would lose his right to appoint people to Church offices forever.

John not only agreed to these terms, he went further and surrendered to the papacy the kingdoms of England and Ireland. From this point onward, he would be the vassal of the pope and hold his kingdoms as fiefs. He also promised an annual payment of 1,000 marks (£675) to the papacy.

As the pope's vassal, he could rely on the support of the papacy if he was attacked. After his reconciliation with John, Innocent withdrew his support for Louis' planned invasion and Louis did not invade England at this time.

Source C

John's agreement with Innocent III was outlined in a charter on 15 May 1213.

We offer and freely yield... to the lord pope Innocent... the whole kingdom of England and the whole kingdom of Ireland... for the remission [forgiveness] of our sins... so that from henceforth we hold them from him and the Roman Church as a vassal... And... we will and decree that from our own income... the Church of Rome shall... receive annually 1000 marks sterling... And if we or any of our successors shall presume to oppose this, let him... forfeit his right in the kingdom. And let this charter of obligation... remain for ever valid.

The terms of John's submission show that he was very worried about the possibility of an invasion and that it was essential to reach an agreement with Innocent to reduce the number of enemies he faced. In fact, the agreement shows that John was a very shrewd politician.

Exam-style question, Section B

'The excommunication of the king was the main consequence of the quarrel between King John and Pope Innocent III in the years 1205–13'.

How far do you agree? Explain your answer.

You may use the following in your answer:

- the Interdict
- royal revenues.

You **must** also use information of your own. **16 marks**

Exam tip

This question is asking you to look at the results of the quarrel between John and Innocent III. When examining the consequences of an event, you should identify at least three results and explain their importance. A good answer will also make links between the consequences and explain which is most important and why.

The spark, 1205–7
- King John quarrels with the Canterbury monks over the appointment of the Archbishop of Canterbury.
- Pope Innocent III puts forward his own candidate, Stephen Langton.
- John refuses to accept Innocent's choice and will not allow Stephen Langton to enter England.

The quarrel worsens, 1208–13
- Innocent places England under an Interdict.
- Some of John's clergy leave England. John collects revenue from their lands.
- John is excommunicated. More clergy leave England and the barons become angry.

The quarrel is settled, 1213
- The threat of a French invasion persuades John to settle the quarrel with the pope.
- John agrees to let Stephen Langton into England and take up his position as archbishop.
- John hands over his kingdom to Innocent and becomes his vassal.

Figure 3.3 A summary of the dispute between John and the papacy, 1206–13.

In July 1213, Stephen Langton arrived in England. After John had made an initial payment of £4,000 to the papacy, Langton lifted the Interdict. The bishops and abbots who had left England during the Interdict were restored to their property and even those who had supported John during the quarrel found that they were rewarded with offices and high income. Innocent now allowed John to choose his own bishops without interference, so the quarrel ended to the satisfaction of both men. Although John had to accept Stephen Langton as Archbishop of Canterbury, the benefits he enjoyed from his new-found friendship with the papacy far outweighed the disadvantages. During the baronial rebellion of 1215–16, John was able to call on the support of the pope against his opponents (see page 84), so the agreement turned out to be a very wise move.

Activity

Design a poster showing the impact of the Interdict on the lives of ordinary people in England. Or, design a poster publicising John's reconciliation with Pope Innocent.

Summary

- King John and Pope Innocent III quarrelled after both men claimed the right to select the Archbishop of Canterbury.
- John refused to accept Innocent's choice of Stephen Langton because he was, in John's view, too closely connected with his French enemies.
- Innocent placed an Interdict on England in 1208, which denied people church services and sacraments.
- When the Interdict failed to force John to submit, Innocent excommunicated him.
- John submitted to Innocent in 1213 to prevent an invasion from France; he made himself the vassal of the pope. John now had the pope's support.

Checkpoint

Strengthen

S1 What is meant by excommunication?

S2 In a sentence, explain how important the Interdict was to ordinary people in England.

S3 Write a paragraph explaining why John decided to submit to Innocent III in 1213.

Challenge

C1 What was the consequence of the Interdict for John's barons and bishops?

C2 Explain why John was reluctant to reach an agreement with Innocent III. Your answer should include at least two reasons.

How confident do you feel about your answers to these questions? If you have any difficulties, re-read pages 69–73 in this section to help you develop your answers.

3.2 Worsening relations with the barons

Learning outcomes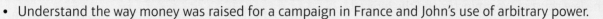

- Understand the way money was raised for a campaign in France and John's use of arbitrary power.
- Understand the plot of 1212 and John's failure to capture Normandy in 1214.

The dispute with the papacy was just one reason why John's relationship with his barons declined from 1205. The loss of Normandy also caused a growing division between the king and his leading vassals. As John sought to raise the money to launch a war of re-conquest in France, so his demands for taxes increased and his methods of extracting the money became more cruel.

John's financial problems

John faced greater problems in financing his government than his brother had done because the economic situation was worsening in the early 13th century.

- There was a steady rise in prices (known as inflation) at this time, which lowered the value of royal income. In other words, the money that the king had could buy less.
- There was a substantial loss of revenues due to the loss of Normandy.

The economic situation meant that John struggled to find the money to fund a war in France, which would include the high cost of hiring mercenaries (professional soldiers). Matters were not improved by John's own spending: in 1205 he spent over £700 on the robes he wore for the Christmas feast. This was a huge sum of money at a time when a typical knights' fee was barely £20 a year.

Extend your knowledge

Inflation in John's reign
The inflation in John's reign was caused by a number of factors. The debasement (see page 26) of coinage happening at this time was lowering its value, leading sellers to demand higher prices. Debasement also led to an increase in the number of silver coins in the country, which again made sellers demand higher prices. On top of this, the population of England was growing, which meant that there was more demand for goods and so sellers could charge more for them.

Interpretation 1

From *King John* (1997) by W.L. Warren. Here Warren describes the impact of John's demands for taxes on his barons.

Inevitably there was persistent grumbling about taxation – the scutages, almost annual under John, the newer taxes on chattels [personal property] and ploughlands, the [feudal incidents] that were only occasional but heavy and sometimes crushing, and about the arbitrarily fixed... fines. But in addition... there can have been few of the hundred and sixty or so tenants-in-chief who had not some personal grievance about royal tyranny, an injury to pride in the destruction of a castle, a sense of injustice in the disposal of a manor, a bitterness about the pillaging of an estate while in wardship, or the indignity of the forced marriage of a widow or an heiress.

One way that John raised money was to impose fines on his barons. For example, he fined one baron £810 and 12 horses for marrying an heiress without the king's licence and seized the lands of both the baron and his new wife. He also commonly charged £405 as a fine on inheriting feudal lands at a time when £100 was regarded as a reasonable payment for this feudal relief. Using methods like this, John was able to raise money, but it is little wonder that his barons regarded his taxation policy as unreasonable.

The use of arbitrary power

The arbitrary* way in which John wielded his power also caused problems. Between 1209 and 1214, John virtually closed down the law court at Westminster and the judicial eyres* in the counties. Only his own approved judges were permitted to hear cases. The barons resented John's control over justice because he applied the law according to his own whims and for his own benefit. John was also accused of selling justice (see page 28).

Key terms

Arbitrary*

Taking action based on a personal whim or prejudice. For example, a king, could be said to use his power in an arbitrary way if, they arrested a person who had angered them, but there was no evidence against that person and the proper process of law was ignored.

Judicial eyre*

This involved a judge from the royal courts visiting the local courts and hearing cases. This was to make sure that the king's justice was being put into practice in the same way across the whole kingdom.

One of the ways in which John's barons fell out with him was by failing to repay their debts. The barons resented the fact that John used their debts to increase his power over them. John's power over the barons is clearly shown by the fate of William de Braose.

William de Braose was one of John's most favoured barons in the early years of his reign and he was

Source A

Anonymous of Béthune, probably writing in the 1220s, describes the death of Lady de Braose and her son in *History of the Dukes of Normandy and the Kings of England*.

On the eleventh day the mother was found dead between her son's legs, still upright but leaning back against her son's chest as a dead woman. The son, who was also dead, sat upright, leaning against the wall as a dead man. So desperate was the mother that she had eaten her son's cheeks. When William de Braose, who was in Paris, heard this news, he died soon afterwards... through grief.

rewarded with lands in England, Wales and Ireland. However, some time in 1207–8, John turned against him, claiming that de Braose owed him money for land that he held. De Braose was ordered to hand over his sons as hostages until the debt was paid. He was chased from his lands and escaped into exile. His wife and eldest son were not so lucky. They were captured and put in prison, where they starved to death (see Source A).

Extend your knowledge

The fate of William and Lady de Braose

The story of William de Braose is often used to illustrate John's cruelty and to explain baronial opposition to him. However, some historians have challenged this depiction of the king. They argue that de Braose had become an over-mighty subject who had incurred debts that he had no intention of paying. John demanded his sons as hostages as security for the unpaid debt.

In the 13th century, it was considered reasonable to take hostages as a guarantee for good behaviour. However, according to Roger of Wendover, Lady de Braose rashly declared that she would not give up her sons to a man who had murdered his nephew (referring to Arthur of Brittany). Lady de Braose acted in bad faith by refusing to hand over her sons and, if she did denounce John, as Roger claims, it is likely that her accusation encouraged John to attempt to seize de Braose and his family.

William de Braose had captured Arthur at Mirebeau and was in Brittany when he was murdered. It was likely that he knew John's role in his death, so his wife's accusation was dangerous to John.

While the barons felt that John was acting unjustly and cruelly, there was little chance of them getting justice. John was the king and therefore the highest authority in terms of justice. John's constant presence in England in the years 1205–14 also meant that it was impossible for the barons to blame 'evil advisers' for their mistreatment, as subjects had done in the past when the king was absent. John's arbitrary use of power, his demands for taxes and fines, and his misuse of the justice system, prompted some barons to plot against him.

The plot of 1212

In the years 1209–12, John led campaigns in Ireland and Wales to take control of the lands that he had granted to William de Braose and to crush any rebel support for his former favourite. However, in the campaign of 1211, the Welsh prince, Llywelyn ap Iorwerth, had seized land for himself and this enraged John. John invaded Wales and forced Llywelyn into submission. He demanded that Llywelyn hand over his son as a hostage as a guarantee of good behaviour, but it was not enough to deter Llywelyn. He made an agreement in 1212 with Philip II to work with the French king against John.

John was preparing to launch an attack on Wales when he learned that Llywelyn was in league with some of his barons who had hatched a plot to kill him. The rebel barons included Eustace de Vesci and Robert Fitz Walter. Fitz Walter owed money to John and, it was claimed, both men were angry about John's attempts to seduce female relations. John was very aware of the seriousness of the situation. He cancelled the Welsh campaign and marched north to re-establish his authority as king (it is likely he held a crown-wearing ceremony in York). Both Fitz Walter and de Vesci fled into exile.

The plot must have called John to question his own behaviour. After defeating the plotters, he did make some concessions including relaxing some of his demands for taxes. It was probably at this time that he decided he needed to make his peace with the pope.

Extend your knowledge

Robert Fitz Walter and Eustace de Vesci

Robert Fitz Walter was one of the most powerful barons in the kingdom. He held 66 knights' fees and he added another 32 knights' fees by marrying an heiress. His reasons for rebellion are not clear. Roger of Wendover claims that Fitz Walter fell out with the king due to a quarrel he was having with the abbot at St Albans priory. But Fitz Walter told the French king that he turned against John when the king attempted to seduce his daughter Mathilda. Other historians point to Fitz Walters' grievances over his debts and his anger that John had not supported his claims to Hertford castle.

Eustace de Vesci was a great landowner in the north of England. He was one of the most important vassals that accompanied John on his campaign in Ireland in 1210. He bitterly disliked John, accusing him of attempting to seduce his wife. He also resented the payments going to John for things like forest fines and scutages. Indeed, like many other barons, he refused to pay the scutage of 1214.

Both de Vesci and Fitz Walter were invited back to England after John had reached the settlement with the pope in 1213.

Source B

The seal of Robert Fitz Walter, the leader of the rebels in the plot against John in 1212. The seal shows Fitz Walter to be a fierce knight.

Activities

1 Write down three reasons why you think John was determined to make his barons pay their fines?

2 With a partner, look back through this chapter and write down a list of all the things that you think might have caused Robert Fitz Walter and Eustace de Vesci to plot against King John. Compare your list with another pair: are there any points that you disagree on?

3 Write a short letter from Robert Fitz Walter to Llywelyn, persuading him to join the plot of 1212.

The impact of the failure to regain Normandy in 1214

John's main focus was on regaining his lands on the continent, and his harsh taxes were to raise funds for a campaign in France. The plot of 1212 and the threat of Prince Louis' invasion in 1213 encouraged John to reach the agreement with the pope; by 1214, he was ready to launch his campaign. If John were to succeed in retrieving his lands, it was possible that his relationship with his barons would improve. Faithful barons would have the chance to gain some reward from a French campaign and the income from Normandy would improve John's financial position. Failure, however, would make it almost impossible for him to restore his relationship with the barons, especially after he had demanded so much from them in taxes and feudal fines.

Defeat at the Battle of Bouvines

In February 1214, John set sail for France. Few of his barons accompanied him, but he did take with him a large treasury, which was described as overflowing with precious gemstones, silver and gold. In total, John is believed to have spent £135,000 on the campaign.

This huge sum had mainly been provided through another scutage (the eleventh of John's reign) and by feudal fines on the barons and knights.

John's carefully planned campaign relied on the support of European allies. Without them, he could not defeat Philip II. On 27 July a battle was fought at Bouvines, where John's main ally, the Holy Roman Emperor, Otto IV, led an army against Philip. Otto's army included some of John's men. Despite outnumbering its enemy, Otto's army was defeated by the French. The defeat was so decisive that it ended any hope John had of restoring Angevin rule in Normandy.

After the battle, John returned to England without anything to show for the heavy taxes that he had taken from the English people and many barons became rebellious. Most historians agree that the scutage of 1214 (raised for the French campaign), and his defeat at Bouvines, led to the baronial rebellion that followed.

Source C

Philip II of France unhorsed at the Battle of Bouvines, 27 July 1214. From a drawing by the 13th-century chronicler Matthew Paris. Although Philip fell from his horse, he went on to win the battle.

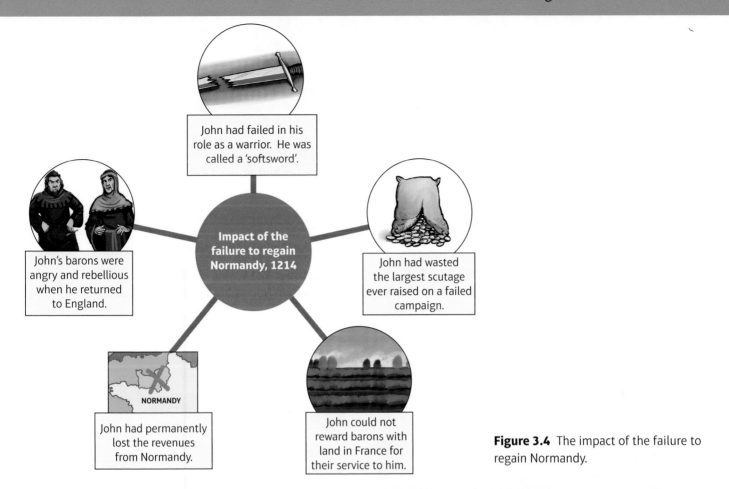

Figure 3.4 The impact of the failure to regain Normandy.

Summary

- John exploited his feudal rights to demand high fines and taxes from his subjects.
- He also used his power in an arbitrary way, causing many barons to view him as unjust.
- In 1212, John discovered that some of his barons were plotting his murder. He crushed the plot and forced the rebels into exile.
- John launched his campaign to recover Normandy in 1214, but it ended in disaster at the Battle of Bouvines.

Checkpoint

Strengthen

S1 List two reasons why the barons resented John's demands for taxes.

S2 What is meant by arbitrary use of power?

S3 What was the impact of the 1212 plot on John's behaviour?

Challenge

C1 Use the material in this section to create a timeline starting in 1205 to trace John's worsening relationship with his barons.

C2 How far can John's treatment of William de Braose and his family be justified? Construct a table with two columns, for and against. Try to write down at least six bullet points in the table as a whole.

How confident do you feel about your answers to these questions? If you are not sure that you answered them well, you could work through them again with a partner.

3.3 Magna Carta and the First Barons' War

On 15 June 1215, at Runnymede, just outside Windsor, King John put his seal to the most famous agreement ever made between an English king and his subjects. This agreement was written up as a great charter, or 'Magna Carta', and distributed in the shires of England. For the first time ever, the king's authority was clearly limited by the law.

Source A

Magna Carta (or Great Charter) – this is one of the four surviving copies of Magna Carta from 1215 and it is kept today in Salisbury Cathedral.

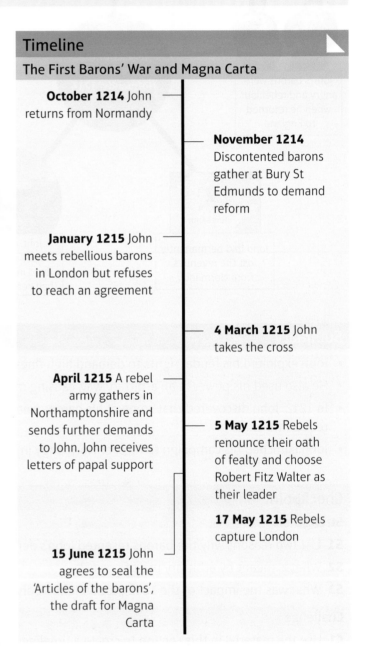

Timeline

The First Barons' War and Magna Carta

October 1214 John returns from Normandy

November 1214 Discontented barons gather at Bury St Edmunds to demand reform

January 1215 John meets rebellious barons in London but refuses to reach an agreement

4 March 1215 John takes the cross

April 1215 A rebel army gathers in Northamptonshire and sends further demands to John. John receives letters of papal support

5 May 1215 Rebels renounce their oath of fealty and choose Robert Fitz Walter as their leader

17 May 1215 Rebels capture London

15 June 1215 John agrees to seal the 'Articles of the barons', the draft for Magna Carta

The rebellion of 1215

John returned from the continent in 1214 to find his barons in a rebellious mood. John's failure in Normandy angered the barons who had paid for the war. Also, in his absence, John's justiciar, Peter des Roches, had further alienated the barons. In particular, he had demanded that the barons who had not joined John on campaign should pay the scutage. This demand was strongly resisted by barons in Yorkshire and, by the time John returned, a distinctive group of rebels had emerged led by Eustace de Vesci (see page 77), along with William de Mowbray and Roger de Montbegon (who were both heavily in debt to John).

Angry barons gathered in November 1214 at Bury St Edmunds. Their aim was to force John to confirm the Coronation Charter* of his great grandfather, Henry I, in which the king promised good government and to respect the customs of the realm*. If John refused, the barons present at the meeting swore to rebel against him.

Key terms

Coronation Charter*

Issued by Henry I in 1100 at his coronation – in the charter he swore an oath to abolish evil customs and restore good government to England. The 'charter of liberties', as it was called, guaranteed the rights of free Englishmen.

Customs of the realm*

The rules for local justice that had existed since Anglo-Saxon times. These rules, or 'customs', had not been written down when they were created and had changed over time. This was a problem because the king and his subjects did not always agree on what the customs were.

John attempted to play for time. In January 1215, he met his barons at a council meeting in London. They expected John to confirm the Coronation Charter, but John refused, saying he would give them a decision on 26 April. John then strengthened his position when he took crusader vows on 4 March. This placed him under the special protection of the Church. Taking these vows also meant that his barons were obliged to avoid any actions that would prevent John from going on crusade.

This meant that John did not have to settle their grievances, and they, in turn, were not allowed to rebel.

To stall the barons further, John sent William Marshal and Stephen Langton to negotiate with them. No agreements were reached and the barons ran out of patience. A rebel army gathered in Northamptonshire in April. About 39 of John's barons and 1,400 knights were in open rebellion against him. Although this represented a significant uprising of John's feudal lords, the rebels were still in the minority, as there were 165 barons in England and 6,500 knights. However, John could not rely on the support of all these other barons and knights, because many of them refused to take a side. The rebels in Northamptonshire made further (unknown) demands on John but, once again, John did not feel under pressure to give in. The letters of support from the papacy that John received in April gave him the confidence to continue to refuse the rebels' demands.

On 5 May, the rebels took more drastic steps as they renounced their oaths of fealty to John and selected Robert Fitz Walter as their leader. They attempted to seize the castle at Northampton, but failed as it was well-defended by royal forces. The rebels then moved on to London, which they captured successfully on 17 May with the help of the Londoners.

The threat to John had grown considerably now that the rebels held the capital city. John had attempted to win the favour of the Londoners a month earlier by granting them the right to choose their own mayor, but it had not been enough to secure their loyalty. The loss of London meant the loss of its finances and this would make it difficult for John to end the war quickly.

Runnymede and Magna Carta

The motives of the barons

Although chroniclers of the period refer to the rebels as '**the northerners**', it is reasonable to suggest that their motivations for rebellion reflected the general discontent amongst the barons and knights class in England. Indeed, about half of the barons who revolted were not from the north at all, they were barons who held lands in the western shires, East Anglia, Essex, and other places.

Figure 3.5 Reasons for the barons' rebellion.

- High taxation – the 1214 scutage especially caused great anger.
- John's aggressive pursuit of his feudal rights, with high fines demanded for inheritance, wardship and the property of widows.

MONEY

POWER

- The declining role of the barons in government – barons were replaced by 'new men' who were appointed by the king. This reduced the barons' power.

TREATMENT

- John's use of arbitrary powers denied justice to knights and barons.
- Accusations that John seduced wives and daughters of some barons.
- Treatment of the de Braose family – barons in debt to John feared similar treatment.

Activities ?

1 Why do you think John rejected the barons' initial demands in January 1215?

2 You and your partner are rebel barons. You should each make lists of the reasons why you oppose King John. Agree four demands that you will put to the king to address the way that he has wronged you.

3 Write King John's reply to the rebels' demands. You may want to refresh your memory about the duties of a baron to their king as well as using information from this chapter.

Source B

The 13th-century chronicler, Roger of Wendover, quotes a speech made by Stephen Langton to the barons in August 1213.

Did you hear how, when I absolved the king at Winchester, I made him swear that he would do away with unjust laws and recall good laws, such as those of King Edward [the Confessor – King of England 1042–1066] and cause them to be observed by all in the kingdom. A charter by Henry I has been found by which you may, if you wish it, recall your long lost rights.

It seems that, even though they had renounced their oath of fealty, the barons were not keen to fight a civil war. John outnumbered them in terms of men and castles, and already he was buying support by offering the lands of rebel barons to those who would back him. He also had the support of the most important baron in England, William Marshal. Rather than war, the rebel barons wanted to limit John's power over them.

Stephen Langton's motives

Stephen Langton was sent by John to negotiate with the rebels, but may well have been sympathetic to them. According to Roger of Wendover, even as early as August 1213, Langton was discussing limitations to the king's powers with the barons (see Source B). Indeed, in the final agreement presented to John, the demand for the freedom of the Church is emphasised and may be evidence that Langton was not an impartial negotiator.

Magna Carta

Negotiations between the rebels and John took place from 27 May, after a truce had been called. A document known as the 'Articles of the barons' was drawn up and, on 10 June, John agreed that this was a basis for a settlement. Five days later (15 June), he rode to Runnymede in Surrey to seal the agreement. Modern images of the event usually show an angry John being forced to agree to the document. However, some historians argue that John was eager to affix his seal to the document. This was because he feared that, if he delayed, he might have been presented with terms that placed greater restrictions on him.

Interpretation 1

Historian Marc Morris gives his opinion on John's eagerness to seal Magna Carta in his book, *King John: Treachery, Tyranny and the Road to Magna Carta* (2015).

John had been staying at Windsor for the duration of the talks, and it is not impossible he made further visits to Runnymede. Certainly he must have been aware of the progress of negotiations from one day to the next, and it seems that after five days he decided that there was no point in prolonging them any further. On 15 June he appeared at Runnymede and shut down the debate by sealing the charter... By sealing Magna Carta, John had batted the issue back into his opponents' camp. The barons now had to decide among themselves whether or not to accept it... Some probably wanted to hold out longer in the hope of obtaining even better terms... But on the content of the charter John stood his ground, and eventually his opponents had to accept that this was the best deal they were going to get.

Once the charter had been sealed, the barons renewed their oaths of fealty and it appeared that the great crisis of John's reign had been resolved.

The main provisions of Magna Carta

The document had 63 clauses, which covered five main areas:

Source C

The seal of King John. An impression of this seal would have been used on Magna Carta.

Key area	Details
The Church	The English Church was to be free; elections were to be free from interference by the king.
Feudal concerns	• The king's demands for aid and scutage were limited. He would only be able to raise such taxes with the agreement of the barons. • A baron's fine on inheriting his lands was set at £100. • John's rights over widows and their dowries were limited.
Justice	The right that the king could not arrest, imprison, outlaw or confiscate the lands of a freeman unless it was done according to the law was established. There had to be a trial by his peers before a sentence was passed. John also promised not to delay or sell justice.
Protection of freemen	• The merchants of London were granted freedom of movement in and out of England to conduct their trade without requiring permission. • Weights and measures were standardised so that buyers knew exactly what they were getting for their money. • The royal forests were limited in size so that fewer subjects would have to pay fines for living and working in them. • The rights of the barons to advise the king were also protected.
Guarantees	A council of 25 barons was to be appointed to share power with the king and to advise him. This would help to guarantee that John would keep his promises.

As soon as it was sealed, Magna Carta was copied by scribes and sent to county courts to be proclaimed to the people. John also sent letters to his officials across the country to announce that peace had been reached and that the rebels had renewed their oaths of fealty.

Clause 14

John promised not to collect scutages and other taxes without the permission of his council of barons.

Clauses 39 and 40

John promised not to sell justice, or imprison or outlaw or fine any freeman unless it was allowed by the law. A freeman could not be sentenced before he had been given a trial by his peers.

Clause 61

John agreed to establish a council of 25 barons who would advise him.

Figure 3.6 A summary of the most important clauses in Magna Carta.

The outbreak of war

John sealed Magna Carta because he wanted to avoid war and because he hoped to attract more supporters to his side. However, he did not want to implement the agreement. Most historians are of the opinion that Magna Carta would never have worked. A key reason for this was the council of 25 barons who were to ensure that John kept his word. These barons would have been chosen from among the rebels and this could never have been acceptable to John.

Shortly after he had put his seal to the document, John contacted the pope. The full benefit of his settlement with the papacy in 1213 now became clear. In August, Innocent III issued a papal bull (see Source D) in which he declared that the charter was illegal because John had been forced to agree to it. He announced that he would excommunicate anyone who tried to make John follow its terms. This gave John the justification he needed to renounce the Charter. It had been in force for just three months.

Source D

Pope Innocent III denounced Magna Carta and annulled it in his papal bull of August 1215.

We utterly reject and condemn this settlement and, under threat of excommunication, we order that the king should not dare to observe it and that the barons and their associates should not require it to be observed. The Charter... we declare to be null and void of all validity for ever.

The barons had had enough. In September, they invited Prince Louis of France to be king of England. Louis had a distant claim to the throne because his wife was a granddaughter of John's father, Henry II. He had also been brought up at court with Arthur of Brittany and so had personal reasons for opposing John. Importantly, Louis could bring with him an army from France to support the barons in their war against John. John, meanwhile, could call upon an army of mercenaries that he had recruited and stationed in Ireland just in case his agreement with the barons failed.

The taking and siege of Rochester

The barons had control of London and were strong in the north and the east, but John did hold a series of castles running up the centre of England and could ensure his control of the west. He also held two castles in rebel territory, Dover and Lincoln. However, he knew that he needed to re-establish control in the south, especially if he was to repel an invasion by Prince Louis.

Rochester castle was one of the most impressive and important fortresses in England. It was situated on the road from London to Dover and this made it of great strategic importance. If John took Rochester, he would make it very hard for Prince Louis to lead an army to London to join with the rebel barons. Therefore, in October, John laid siege to Rochester castle. John had always been greatly skilled at siege warfare. He destroyed the bridges to the castle and cut off the defenders inside. He then instructed his engineers to build five great stone-throwing machines, which were used to bombard the walls. Meanwhile, John's men tunnelled under the walls of one of the towers to undermine its foundations and cause it to collapse. After seven weeks, on 30 November 1215, the castle's inhabitants surrendered to John.

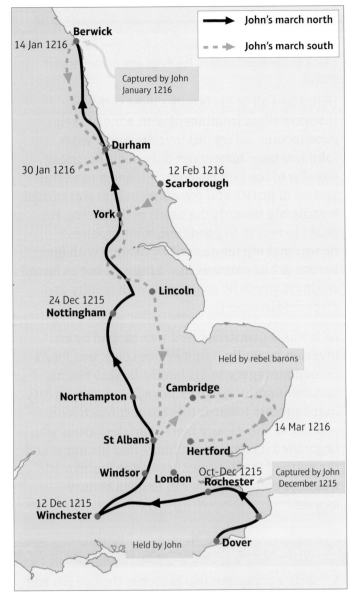

Figure 3.7 A map showing John's campaign against the rebels, September 1215–March 1216. By covering so much ground in such a short period of time, John was able to gain control over most of the country.

Once he had taken Rochester, John quickly moved north. The rebels had gained the support of the Scottish king, Alexander II, by promising him land in the north of England. Alexander had moved south, taking homage from barons in Northumberland and even some in Yorkshire. However, John reacted by recovering the

castle at Berwick in January 1216, before turning south again to deal with the rebels. He took a route through East Anglia, burning down the strongholds of his enemies and taking their castles. By the spring of 1216, John could be forgiven for considering his position in England to be secure. Only London still held out against him.

THINKING HISTORICALLY | **Cause and Consequence (3c&d)**

Causation and intention

1 Work on your own or with a partner to identify as many causes of the outbreak of the First Barons' War as you can. Write each cause on a separate card or piece of paper.

2 Divide your cards into those that represent:

   a the actions or intentions of people

   b the beliefs held by people at the time

   c the contextual factors, e.g. political, social or economic events

   d states of affairs (long-term situations that have developed over time).

3 Focus on the intentions and actions of the key people in the run-up to the outbreak of war: King John, Robert Fitz Walter, Stephen Langton, a rebellious baron. For each person, draw on your knowledge to fill in a table, identifying:

   a their intentions in 1215

   b the actions they took to achieve these

   c the consequences of their actions (both intended and unintended)

   d the extent to which their intentions were achieved.

4 Discuss the following questions with a partner:

   a Did any one party intend for war to break out in 1215?

   b How important are people's intentions, in explaining the outbreak of the First Barons' War?

The invasion of Prince Louis

Prince Louis landed on the south coast on 21 May 1216. His army included several French noblemen and 1,200 knights. John feared meeting this army in battle. Louis immediately retook Rochester castle. Next, he moved on to London, where cheering crowds turned out to greet him, and then to Winchester. The tide had now turned against John.

Some of John's closest supporters believed the king would be defeated and they began to defect to the rebel side. Even his half-brother, the earl of Salisbury, switched sides. In August, King Alexander captured Carlisle before marching south to do homage to Prince Louis in September 1216.

The death of King John

In September, John moved north to relieve his sheriff at Lincoln castle, which was under siege from rebel forces. By this time, John was seriously ill. On his return south from Lincoln, he crossed the marshlands of the Wash in East Anglia. The final humiliation of his reign was the loss of his baggage train*, which sank into the mud. It was claimed that John lost a great deal of treasure, including, as legend has it, the Crown Jewels*. Afterwards, John rested at the abbey at Newark and died on the night of 18 October 1216.

Few mourned John's death. He was an unpopular king then, and his reputation has not changed much since the 13th century. However, more recently, some historians have argued that circumstances were against him. In particular, they emphasise that John suffered from a shortage of money because of Richard's crusade and wars. Moreover, he faced a strong and cunning French king who was determined to expand his territory at John's expense.

Key terms

Baggage train*

A train of wagons that carried the equipment, provisions and valuables of an army on the march.

Crown Jewels*

The crown, and other jewels and ceremonial objects, that the king would wear or carry on important occasions.

Interpretation 2

Dan Jones assesses the extent to which John failed as a king in *The Plantagenets; The Kings who made England* (2012).

[John] had all of his family's most ruthless instincts allied [combined] with none of their good fortune... [Yet for] four deceptive years, John had been master not only of his kingdom, but also of the English church... and a powerful system of justice and government that was turned mercilessly towards the needs of the Crown. He failed to realise in good time what problems he was making for himself by dealing with his barons not as partners in... kingship, but as forced creditors whom he could treat with cruelty and disdain [disrespect].

As it was, a disastrous civil war, capped by an invasion by Philip II and Prince Louis, was John's immediate legacy to his family. In 1215 Magna Carta was nothing more than a failed peace treaty in the process towards this bitter conflict. John was not to know – any more than the barons who negotiated its terms with him – that his name and the myth of the document sealed at Runnymede would be bound together in English history forever.

Activities

1 Write a paragraph that describes the civil war and John's death.

2 How far is it fair to call John a 'bad' king? Working in a group, draw up a list of evidence that would support this claim. Then draw up a list of evidence to challenge it. Remember to look back to Chapter 1 to review the duties and expectations of a medieval king. You should also remind yourselves of the duties of barons to their king.

3 Imagine that John was put on trial in September 1216, accused of failing in his duty as king. Split your class into two groups. One group should put forward the case for prosecution while the other should prepare John's defence. Your teacher can act as the judge and jury.

Source E

King John's tomb in Worcester Cathedral. John is the only Angevin king buried in England.

Summary

- On his return from France, John was faced by a rebellion of 39 of his barons and 1,400 knights who renounced their oath of fealty to him. The rebels captured London and demanded that John give in to their demands.
- John agreed to seal Magna Carta at Runnymede in June 1215; the terms limited his rights to raise taxes and use of arbitrary powers. It also proposed that a council of 25 barons would share power with John.
- Three months later, the pope annulled Magna Carta and civil war broke out between John and his barons.
- John captured Rochester castle and attacked rebel strongholds in the north and east.
- The rebel barons were supported by King Alexander II of Scotland, who invaded England from the north, and Prince Louis of France, who they invited to become king.
- King John died in Newark in October 1216.

Checkpoint

Strengthen

S1 List three reasons why the barons rebelled.

S2 What did Magna Carta say about the king's role in the justice system?

S3 What did John do after he had sealed Magna Carta?

Challenge

C1 Magna Carta has been called a 'baron's charter'. Identify the terms that would benefit the barons and the terms that would benefit ordinary people. (There might be some overlap.)

C2 Explain why the barons offered the crown to Prince Louis.

How confident do you feel about your answers to these questions? If you are stuck on any of these, join with a partner and discuss your ideas. Use this discussion as the starting point for developing your answers.

3.4 The succession

The problem of the succession

John's death had a significant impact on the development of the civil war. He left behind his nine-year-old son, Henry, as his heir. In his will, John entrusted the care of the kingdom to a council of 13 barons who were given the task of restoring control over England. The most important of these barons was William Marshal. John wanted William Marshal to care for Henry and rule for him until he was old enough to rule alone. This request was in recognition of Marshal's great loyalty to the Angevin dynasty and to John in particular.

William Marshal first arranged the funeral of King John, and then turned to the coronation of Henry. It was traditional for kings to be crowned in London at Westminster Abbey. However, London was in rebel hands and it was important to crown Henry sooner rather than later in order to establish his rightful claim to the throne. There was a real danger that the rebels would crown Louis as king. Louis was a strong candidate to be king. He was an adult, a warrior and he had the Kingdom of France behind him. Henry was much weaker by comparison.

Henry was brought to Gloucester and crowned by Peter des Roches, the bishop of Winchester, on 28 October. A circlet of gold, that his mother had worn on her arm, was used as the crown (John's crown had been lost). Henry swore the traditional oaths, saying that he would give justice to his people, and abolish bad laws and customs. He also did homage to the pope for his kingdom and put England under the protection of the Church. This was important because it undermined the rebels. Prince Louis did not have the blessing of the Church and the rebels had no real grounds for a quarrel with King Henry except for the fact that he was John's son.

Source A

The coronation of Henry III illustrated in a 13th-century manuscript. Although Henry was only nine years old when he was crowned, he has been drawn as an adult.

The role of William Marshal as Protector

William Marshal headed Henry's government as the king's **Protector**. He was the natural choice, not just because he was a great landowner (he was Lord of Chepstow, Pembroke and Leinster), but also because he was a calculating general and a shrewd politician. The position itself was unknown in England. There had never been a Protector before, so Marshal's exact powers were uncertain. What was understood was that Marshal would take charge of the government's finances and the campaigns against the rebels. He was supported by the papal legate*, who had just arrived from Rome. As a result of John's settlement with the pope in 1213, the papal legate had superior authority in England than Marshal, but he did not undermine Marshal's authority in directing the recovery of the kingdom.

Key term

Papal legate*

A personal representative of the pope who possesses the authority to act on behalf of the pope in the nation to which he has been sent.

The presence of the papal legate strengthened the king's side. It deprived Louis of the Church's support. Without this, no churchman would take the risk of crowning him. This was a crucial factor in Henry's campaign – the rebels did not have a king.

One of Marshal's first acts as Protector was to reissue a revised version of Magna Carta. This now had the approval of the Church and further undermined the rebels. They had started the civil war because John annulled Magna Carta, but now that Magna Carta had been restored there was no reason for the rebellion to continue. Henry's side had as much to gain from the reissuing of the Charter as the rebels did. Henry's councillors were also great barons, and even Marshal had suffered at John's hands.

Interpretation 1

Historian David Carpenter in his book *The Struggle for Mastery* (2004) explains the importance of the reissuing of Magna Carta in 1216.

John had demanded that all those submitting to him forswear the Charter. Now the regent and Guala [the papal legate], with no time to consult the pope, executed a momentous volte-face [about-turn]. In November 1216 they issued in the king's name, under their own seals (Henry's had yet to be introduced), a revised version of Magna Carta… The regent, like the rest of John's baronial supporters, had as much to gain from the Charter as the barons on the other side. The hope, of course, was that the latter, their cause conceded, would now return to the Angevin camp.

William Marshal faced an uphill struggle in securing Henry's position on the throne. The treasury was empty because John had not been able to collect taxes once the civil war had broken out. Marshal's forces were also too small to risk a battle with the rebel forces and the civil war had encouraged both the Scottish and Welsh lords to seize territory on the English side of their borders. Nevertheless, in spite of these problems, the death of John had undermined the rebels. Now Prince Louis appeared to be trying to steal the throne from the rightful king and some of his supporters switched sides. By 1217, Marshal had succeeded in taking back control of key areas like Lincoln and London, and Prince Louis returned to France.

The condition of England by 1216

The condition of England in 1216 did not look good for several reasons.

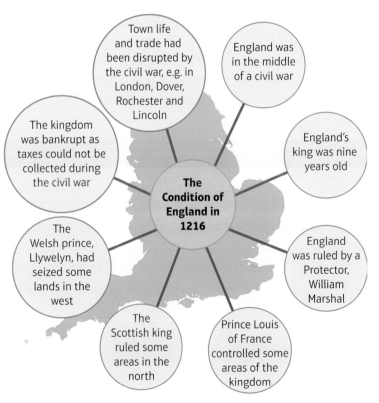

Figure 3.8 The condition of England in 1216.

By 1216, England was much weaker than it was in 1189 and a lot had changed in the country during that time. There is a summary of some of the key developments in the reigns of Richard and John on page 90.

Key developments	Details
The role and authority of the king	• The king had been challenged by the barons. Magna Carta limited the king's power. • In 1216, England's king was a child, not a strong warrior like Richard. Government was in the hands of a Protector and loyal barons.
The position of the barons	• The barons' role had been undermined by 'new men' chosen by the king. • The barons were made to feel vulnerable by John's arbitrary use of power and his cruel punishments. They were also weakened by paying heavy feudal fines and taxes. • However, the barons' position was strengthened by Magna Carta. Those that helped King Henry became more powerful than before.
The role of the knights	• The knights continued to be the most important part of the feudal army, but increasingly the king preferred scutage money to pay for mercenaries.
Financial management	• The crusade and Richard's ransom cost the country a lot of money. The loss of Normandy and the civil war reduced the king's income further. By the end of this period, royal income fell to £8,000 a year, which was a third of John's income in 1199. • Heavy taxes were imposed on all members of society.
The Angevin Empire	• In 1189, the Angevin Empire stretched from Northumbria to the Pyrenees. • By 1216, control had been lost, or largely lost, in Brittany, Normandy, Maine, Anjou, Touraine and Poitou.
The lives of ordinary people	• Heavy taxes and price rises meant that most people would have felt poorer in 1216 compared to 1189. • Magna Carta provided some benefits for freemen in the towns, including freedom to travel in and out of the country to conduct trade, but little changed for most people.

Summary

- William Marshal was made England's Protector and regent when the nine-year-old Henry became king.
- Henry III was crowned at Gloucester and did homage to the pope to secure support of the Church.
- William Marshal reissued Magna Carta; this undermined the position of the rebels.
- Royal authority in England in 1216 was severely limited; parts of the north had been seized by the Scottish king; the western border had been attacked by the Welsh; and Prince Louis of France was occupying London.
- The impact of Richard and John's wars had left England bankrupt by 1216.

Checkpoint

Strengthen

S1 Write a paragraph explaining why William Marshal reissued Magna Carta in 1216.

S2 Describe three ways in which the role of the king had changed by 1216.

Challenge

C1 The government of England changed a lot between 1189 and 1216. Draw up a table with two columns. On one side, note down the key changes. On the other side, list the ways in which the government remained the same. You can use the material in Chapter 1 (pages 23–29) to help you with this.

How confident do you feel about your answers to these questions? Ask your teacher for some hints.

Exam-style question, Section B

Explain why England was in a weak condition by 1216.

You may use the following in your answer:

- the Barons' War
- Henry III

You **must** also use information of your own. **12 marks**

Exam tip

This is a causation question, so you are being asked to explain why something happened. You should try to develop three reasons by providing some detailed information for each reason. This can be developed with an explanation of why each reason was important. A good explanation will also show the links between the reasons.

Recall quiz

1. What was the name of the pope with whom John came into conflict?
2. What was the Interdict?
3. List two reasons why the pope excommunicated John.
4. How many scutages did John demand between 1199 and 1215?
5. What happened to the wife and eldest son of William de Braose?
6. How many barons rebelled against John in 1215?
7. Give one reason why John agreed to seal Magna Carta.
8. What restrictions did Magna Carta place on the king's right to raise taxes?
9. Which castle in the south of England did John capture in December 1215?
10. List three factors that made England a weak country by 1216.

Activities

1. Draw up a table with two columns. On one side, list all the grievances that the barons had against John. On the other side, list the terms in Magna Carta that addressed those grievances.
2. John's relationship with the Church changed a lot during this period. Explain the reasons why John changed from being an enemy of the Church to a favourite.
3. Historians who are sympathetic to John have suggested that his downfall was because circumstances were against him. How true is this opinion? Organise a debate in your class. You will need to gather evidence either for or against the view.
4. You are a medieval chronicler. Write an account of the events in England in the years 1215–16.
   You may include:
   a. the reasons for the outbreak of the civil war
   b. Magna Carta and its annulment
   c. John's death and the succession of Henry III.

Exam-style question, Section B

'King John's use of arbitrary power was the main reason for the barons' rebellion in May-June 1215'.

How far do you agree? Explain your answer.

You may use the following in your answer:

- William de Braose taxes.

You **must** also use information of your own. **16 marks**

Exam tip

This question is about causation. You should identify one or two more reasons for the barons' rebellion. Give some details for each reason to explain how the reason contributed to the outbreak of the rebellion. Try to explain which reason was of the greatest importance.

Writing historically: writing cohesively

When you explain events and their consequences, you need to make your explanation as clear and succinct as possible.

Learning outcomes

By the end of this lesson, you will understand how to:

- use pronouns to refer back to ideas earlier in your writing
- use sentence structures to help you refer back to ideas earlier in your writing clearly and economically.

Definition

Pronoun: a word that can stand in for, and refer back to, a noun, e.g. 'he', 'she', 'this', 'that', etc.

How can I refer back to earlier ideas as clearly as possible?

Look at the beginning below of a response to this exam-style question:

> The excommunication of the king was the main consequence of the quarrel between King John and Pope Innocent III in the years 1205–13. **(16 marks)**

> *The pope put England under an Interdict and then excommunicated King John when John refused Langton entry. This meant that his subjects did not have to obey him.*

1. In the second sentence, the **pronoun** 'this' refers back to the first sentence. What could it refer back to?

   a. the Interdict   **b.** the excommunication   **c.** John's refusal   **d.** it's not clear – it could be referring to any of them.

One way in which you can improve the clarity of your writing is to avoid imprecise pronouns like 'this' and either:

- repeat the idea you are referring back to OR
- replace it with a word or phrase that summarises the idea.

2. Which of these would you choose to replace 'this' to make these sentences as clear and precise as possible?

   a. Excommunication   **b.** The pope's reaction   **c.** These acts   **d.** The Church's stance.

> *The pope put England under an Interdict and then excommunicated King John when John refused Langton entry. This meant that his subjects did not have to obey him.*

3. Now look at some more sentences from the same response below. What could you replace 'This' with to make the sentences as clear as possible?

> The excommunication actually helped John because he could claim revenues from vacant Church offices, while his subjects remained loyal to protect their lands, even though they could not attend services. This improved royal revenues for John who was always short of money.

How can I structure my sentences to make referring back even clearer?

4. Look at the three versions below of sentences written in response to the exam-style question on the previous page:

Version A

> Relations improved after the final settlement, because John was able to appoint his own bishops. This was significant because the pope later supported John over Magna Carta.

The pronoun 'this' is meant to refer back to this phrase – but, because it follows this clause, the writer seems to be suggesting that the pope supported John because John could appoint his own bishops.

Version B

> Because John was able to appoint his own bishops, relations improved after the final settlement. This was significant because the pope later supported John over Magna Carta.

Version C

> Because John was able to appoint his own bishops, relations improved after the final settlement. This reconciliation was significant because the pope later supported John over Magna Carta.

Which version is most clearly expressed and therefore easiest to read?
Write a sentence or two explaining your ideas, thinking about:

- the use of the pronoun 'this'
- the position of the idea it refers back to
- the use of a word or phrase that summarises the idea.

Did you notice?

When you read a text, you usually assume that the pronoun 'this' refers back to the piece of information that you have just read – not the one before that, or the one two or three sentences ago.

5. Why are the sentences below unclear and difficult to make sense of?

> In 1209, the pope excommunicated King John. His subjects no longer had to obey him and his authority was reduced. This cut him off from the Church and damned his soul to hell.

Improving an answer

6. Experiment with two or three different ways of rearranging and/or rewriting the sentence fragments below to create sentences that explain as clearly as possible why John's financial problems were aided by his excommunication.

> [1] John claimed clerical revenues [2] when he was excommunicated [3] because 17 abbots and 7 bishops left the country [4] This eased his financial problems.

Preparing for your GCSE Paper 2 exam

Paper 2 overview

Your Paper 2 is in two sections that examine the Period Study and British Depth Study. They each count for 20% of your History assessment. The questions on King Richard I and King John are the British Depth Study and are in Section B of the exam paper. You should save just over half the time allowed for Paper 2 to write your answers to Section B. This will give a few moments for checking your answers at the end.

History Paper 2	Period Study and British Depth Study			Time 1 hour 45 mins
Section A	Period Study	Answer 3 questions	32 marks	50 mins
Section B	Medieval Depth Option B2	Answer 3 questions	32 marks	55 mins

British Depth Option B2 The reigns of King Richard I and King John, 1189–1216

You will answer Question 5, which is in three parts:

(a) Describe two features of... (4 marks)

You are given a few lines to write about each feature. Allow five minutes to write your answer. It is only worth four marks, so keep the answer brief and not try to add more information on extra lines.

(b) Explain why... (12 marks)

This question asks you to explain the reasons why something happened. Allow 20 minutes to write your answer. You are given two stimulus (information) points as prompts to help you. You do not have to use the prompts and you will not lose marks by leaving them out. Always remember to add in a new point of your own as well. Higher marks are gained by adding in a point extra to the prompts. You will be given at least two pages in the answer booklet for your answer. This does not mean you should try to fill all the space. The front page of the exam paper tells you 'there may be more space than you need'. Aim to give at least three explained reasons.

(c)(i) OR (ii) How far do you agree? (16 marks)

This question is worth half of your marks for the whole of the British Depth Study. Make sure you have kept 30 minutes to answer it. You have a choice of statements: (i) or (ii). Before you decide, be clear what the statement is about: what 'concept' it is about and what topic information you will need to respond to it. You will have prompts to help as for part (b).

The statement can be about the concepts of: cause, significance, consequence, change, continuity, similarity or difference. It is a good idea during revision to practise identifying the concept focus of statements. You could do this with everyday examples and test one another: *the bus was late because it broke down = statement about cause; the bus broke down as a result of poor maintenance = statement about consequence; the bus service has improved recently = statement about change.*

You must make a judgement on **how far you agree** and you should think about **both** sides of the argument. Plan your answer before you begin to write and put your answer points in two columns: For and Against. You should consider at least three points. Think about it as if you were putting weight on each side to decide what your judgement is going to be for the conclusion. That way your whole answer hangs together – it is coherent. Be clear about your reasons (your criteria) for your judgement – for example why one cause is more important than another? Did it perhaps set others in motion? You must **explain** your answer.

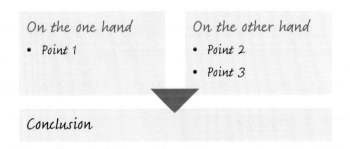

On the one hand
- Point 1

On the other hand
- Point 2
- Point 3

Conclusion

Paper 2, Question 4a

Describe **two** features of kingship at the end of the 12th century. **(4 marks)**

Developed points.

> **Exam tip**
>
> Keep your answer brief. Two points with some extra information about each feature is all you need.

Average answer

A medieval king needed to be a strong warrior to keep his kingdom safe from attack.

A medieval king was anointed with holy oil at his coronation.

> Identifies two features but without any supporting information.

Verdict

This is an average answer because it identifies two valid features of kingship but has not provided any supporting information to develop the features.

• Use the feedback to rewrite this answer, making as many improvements as you can.

Strong answer

A medieval king needed to be a strong ruler to keep his kingdom safe from attack. For example, Richard I was a great warrior who successfully defended his lands in Normandy from attacks by the French king, Philip II.

A medieval king was anointed with holy oils at his coronation. This showed that he had been chosen by God and held divine authority so that he could not be questioned by his subjects.

> The answer has identified a feature – a quality needed by a medieval king – and has supported it with information that is directly related to it.

> The answer has identified a feature – a nature of the authority of a medieval king – and has supported it with information that further develops the understanding of that feature.

Verdict

This is a strong answer because two valid features are given with supporting information.

Paper 2, Question 4b

Explain why men joined the Third Crusade.
You may use the following in your answer:
- indulgences
- financial gains.

You **must** also use information of your own. **(12 marks)**

Average answer

Many men went to fight in the Third Crusade after they were promised a full indulgence for taking part. The indulgence was promised by the pope. It meant that they would be forgiven for their sins and would go to heaven when they died. The crusade was seen as a 'just war' and the Church approved of men going to the Holy Land to fight. The aim of the Third Crusade was to regain Christian control of the Holy Land, and especially of Jerusalem.

The information here is relevant and accurate. There is an explanation of what an indulgence was and there are some hints about its role in encouraging men to go on crusade. However, there is more description than explanation of the key point: men who fought and died on crusade believed they would not go to purgatory to be 'purged' of their sins but would gain immediate entry to heaven.

Some men who joined the crusade wanted to make financial gains. They wanted to get richer, and in the Holy Land there was a chance that they could gain some land and this would give them power and wealth.

The information given here is relevant and is directly linked to the stimulus points. However, it is rather generalised and should be focused more on explanation than description.

In addition, the English army that went to the Holy Land included Welsh bowmen, squires and leading churchmen. There were camp followers too, who were often the wives and families of the knights, and they performed duties like cooking and caring for the sick.

This introduces new information and some of it has relevance but the question asks why men joined the crusade. The information about wives and families cannot be rewarded.

Verdict

This is an average answer because:
- the information is accurate and shows a knowledge and understanding of the topic
- it adds an additional point to the stimulus material which means it is not a weak answer
- it describes rather than explains so it is not a strong answer
- the development of the material is rather generalised in places and the lines of reasoning are not clear.

Use this feedback to rewrite the answer, making as many improvements as you can.

Paper 2, Question 4b

Explain why men joined the Third Crusade. **(12 marks)**

Strong answer

Religious reasons were very important in motivating men to join the Third Crusade. Crusaders were promised an indulgence by Pope Gregory VIII in 1187 when he called upon Christians to rescue the Holy Land from the Muslims. An indulgence meant that a knight would have immediate entry to heaven upon his death without having to spend any time in purgatory being 'purged' of his sins. This was an attractive incentive for knight to join the crusade, especially as life as a knight was dangerous and the threat of death was constant. Medieval warriors feared for their souls and the promise of salvation on their death was very appealing.

> This is a focused paragraph, which explains what an indulgence was and explains why it would encourage men to join the crusade.

Another very important reason for joining the crusade was financial. The knights who took part did not have to pay the Saladin tithe, and they also had the chance to gain land in the crusader states. This was a very important reason for the younger sons of lords and knights to join the crusade. Their older brothers would inherit the family lands, so, if younger sons wanted to be wealthy landowners, they needed to find land elsewhere. The Holy Land was one place where they could gain land as a reward for fighting well.

> This paragraph has a valid point and develops both the specific information and the explanation well.

Members of a knight's military household owed service to their lords and were expected to accompany them on campaigns. This group included squires who were the servants of the knights and were training to become knights. In addition, Richard I recruited valuable professional fighters like Welsh bowmen who were skilled in battle and who fought in return for a fee. These professional soldiers and members of military households took part in the crusade because they owed service to their lords, they had the chance to gain glory or because they were paid to go.

> This paragraph introduces an additional point and has some developed and relevant information. It is not quite as well-focused on explanation as the previous two paragraphs but it is tied to the question.

Verdict

This is a strong answer because:
- there is a good range of information that has been selected specifically to address the question
- the explanation is analytical and it is directed to answer the question.

Paper 2, Question 4c

'The excommunication of the king was the main consequence of the quarrel between King John and Pope Innocent III in the years 1205–13'. How far do you agree? Explain your answer.
You may use the following in your answer:
- the Interdict
- royal revenues.

You **must** also use information of your own. **(16 marks)**

Exam tip

Consider points for and against the statement and make a judgement. Be clear about your reasons for agreeing or disagreeing.

Average answer

King John quarrelled with the pope over who had the right to appoint the Archbishop of Canterbury. He refused to allow Pope Innocent III's choice of Stephen Langton to enter England so Innocent first put England under an Interdict and then, in 1209, he excommunicated John. This meant that his barons and bishops were expected to avoid him and his subjects did not have to obey him. People who were excommunicated were cut off from the Church and were thought to go to hell. The pope excommunicated John because he wanted to force him to obey and nothing had worked up to that point.

During John's quarrel with the pope, some churchmen went abroad and so John left their positions vacant, which meant he could claim their income. John actually became richer during his quarrel with the pope. There were 17 abbacies and seven bishoprics that were left without their head and John could claim all of their income. This actually meant that he was better off by not ending the quarrel with the pope.

John settled his quarrel with the pope in 1213 because he was worried about an invasion from France. He agreed to pay the Pope £27,000 and to become his vassal. He also agreed to let Stephen Langton become the Archbishop of Canterbury. Overall, the excommunication was the main consequence of the quarrel.

The information provided here is accurate and relevant. However, it is used in a rather narrative way. There is a link to the question in the last line that implies that excommunication was the main consequence, but this needs to be made more explicit.

The information here is accurate and relevant and there is a line of reasoning developed although it could be made clearer.

This introduces a new point and is both relevant and accurate but is used descriptively. A judgement is given but it is not developed or explained.

Verdict

This is an average answer because:
- it shows knowledge and understanding of the topic and adds a point in addition to the stimulus material so it is not a weak answer
- it is more descriptive than analytical
- it states a judgement but this is not explained sufficiently for it to be a strong answer.

Use the feedback given here to rewrite this answer, making as many improvements as you can.

Paper 2, Question 4c

'The excommunication of the king was the main consequence of the quarrel between King John and Pope Innocent III in the years 1205–13'. How far do you agree? Explain your answer. **(16 marks)**

Strong answer

The excommunication of King John in 1209 could be seen as the most important consequence of his quarrel with Pope Innocent III, which had started when John refused to accept Stephen Langton as Archbishop of Canterbury. Excommunication is the most serious punishment used by the Church. It meant that John was completely cut off from the Church and that he was thought to be damned to hell. His subjects also did not have to obey him and this was very serious, as it meant they did not have to perform their feudal duties. This reduced John's authority and the pope expected that it would force John to obey him. However, it was not as effective as Innocent III had intended. More of John's churchmen left the country, but overall, most of his subjects remained loyal because they did not want to lose their lands. This meant that John was largely able to ignore the excommunication. It did not have any more impact on him than the Interdict (in place since 1208), which had cut his people off from church services and sacraments. After John's excommunication it still took four more years before the quarrel ended, which suggests that the excommunication was not its main consequence.

> This is a strong paragraph. It has relevant and accurate knowledge and a clear line of reasoning. There is developed analysis and judgement.

Another consequence of the quarrel was that John could claim the revenues from the vacant Church offices of churchmen who had left the country. This included 17 abbacies and seven bishoprics. John was always short of money, so this situation also meant he had no incentive to end the quarrel. The excommunication actually made it easier for him to claim more money. This suggests that the excommunication was a more important consequence than royal revenues because it was the excommunication that helped to increase them.

> This is a focused paragraph with some accurate information and an attempt to compare the importance of consequences.

It could be argued that the most important consequence of the quarrel was the final settlement with Pope Innocent III in 1213. John finally agreed to reach a settlement because he was worried that Prince Louis of France was planning to invade and that the pope would support the invasion. He made himself the vassal of the pope, agreed to pay £27,000 and allowed Stephen Langton to take up the position of Archbishop of Canterbury. This agreement was important because after it had been made, John was allowed to appoint his bishops and, in 1215, the pope supported him over Magna Carta. Therefore, although all the consequences are important, the most important consequence was the final settlement because it had a more long lasting impact.

> This is a strong paragraph which introduces a new point and supports it well. There is a focus on analysis and a clear judgement is provided. However, it would be stronger if it had referred explicitly to the given factor of excommunication in weighing up the importance of the consequences.

Verdict

This is a strong answer because:
- there are a wide range of points that are well supported with accurate information
- the factors are analysed and their importance is evaluated
- there is a clear line of reasoning and the judgements are supported with clear criteria.

Answers to Recall Quiz questions

Chapter 1

1 A system that organised the whole of society into a hierarchy based upon the holding of land in return for services.
2 The duty that knights owed to their lord in return for holding their land.
3 A peasant who belonged to his lord. Villeins were not free and could not move to another village.
4 A principle of succession by which the eldest son inherits the father's title and all his lands.
5 Any two reasonable answers, e.g.: i) to keep the peace; ii) to protect his people; iii) to punish excessive greed; iv) to maintain justice.
6 William Longchamp
7 Any two reasonable answers, e.g.: i) John was rash and short tempered; ii) Arthur had committed treason; iii) some regarded Arthur's claim to the throne as better than John's.
8 Any three reasonable answers, e.g.: i) John had Arthur murdered; ii) John treated people cruelly, such as allowing Lady de Braose and her son to starve to death in prison; iii) John imposed high taxes; iv) John chose 'new men' rather than barons to give him advice; v) John was accused of selling justice.
9 A payment made by the holders of a knight's fee in return for not having to fight in his army.
10 Any reasonable answer, e.g.: i) customs duties; ii) collecting tolls; iii) paying the king for a licence for a fair.

Chapter 2

1 A holy war fought by Christians.
2 Any three reasonable answers, e.g.: i) the promise of a full indulgence; ii) to gain land in the Holy Land; iii) to achieve Christian control of the Holy Land; iv) to fulfil their feudal duty by serving in their lord's army; v) to gain wealth; vi) to have their debts cancelled; vii) to avoid paying the 'Saladin tithe'.
3 The Muslim leader in the Holy Land
4 Any three reasonable answers, e.g.: i) Philip II was jealous of the reception that Richard received in Sicily; ii) Richard married Berengaria of Narvarre instead of Philip II's sister Alice; iii) Richard refused to share the spoils of the conquest of Cyprus with Philip; iv) they argued over the candidate for king of Jerusalem.
5 A three-year truce in the fighting during which Christians would have safe access to Jerusalem.
6 Leopold of Austria
7 100,000 marks or £66,000
8 Any reasonable answer, e.g.: it was built high above the town, so it was difficult to tunnel under its walls; it had round walls that were difficult to break with catapults.
9 Any reasonable answer, e.g.: Hugh de Lusignan appealed to Philip II for justice; Philip was able to declare John's lands as forfeit; Arthur did homage for John's Angevin lands in France.
10 Philip was now able to overrun the whole of Normandy.

Chapter 3

1 Innocent III
2 A very serious punishment imposed on England in 1208 by Innocent III. It meant that the people of England were denied access to the Christian sacraments and church services.
3 Any two reasonable answers, e.g.: i) John refused to obey the pope and accept Stephen Langton as Archbishop of Canterbury; ii) the Interdict was not enough to pressurise John into obeying the pope; iii) it would mean John's subjects would not have to obey him and put pressure on John to reconcile with the pope.
4 11
5 They starved to death in one of John's prisons.
6 39
7 Any reasonable answer, e.g.: He feared that the barons might impose worse conditions on him if he delayed; he believed it would not last long because the pope would support him against the rebel barons; he wanted to avoid war; he hoped it would attract more supporters to his side.
8 He would only be able to raise taxes with the agreement of the barons.
9 Rochester
10 Any three reasonable answers, e.g.: i) its king was a minor; ii) it was in the middle of a civil war; iii) it was occupied by Prince Louis of France; iv) the Scottish and Welsh leaders had seized territory on the English side of their borders; v) the kingdom was bankrupt; vi) town life and trade had been disrupted.

Index

Acknowledgements

Picture credits
The publisher would like to thank the following for their kind permission to reproduce their photographs:

(Key: b-bottom; c-centre; l-left; r-right; t-top)

akg-images Ltd: British Library 42, Purkiss Archive 25; **Alamy Images:** Classic Image 26, Esther Smith 80, f8 archive 24, Graham Oliver 34, Heritage Image Partnership Ltd 15, 19, Lebrecht Music and Arts Photo Library 77, 78, PBL Collection 83, Ray Roberts 8, 16, robertharding 87, The Art Archive 6, 7bl, 52, 69, The Print Collector 51 Tim Gartside Travel 61; **Bridgeman Art Library Ltd:** Chapel of St. Radegund, Chinon, France / De Agostini Picture Library 62, Hirmer Fotoarchiv 11, Pictures from History 50; **Mary Evans Picture Library:** INTERFOTO / Sammlung Rauch 7br, 68, 88; **TopFoto:** The Granger Collection 30, Topham Picturepoint 40, 43

Cover images: *Front:* **Alamy Images:** Ryhor Bruyeu

All other images © Pearson Education

Every effort has been made to trace the copyright holders and we apologise in advance for any unintentional omissions. We would be pleased to insert the appropriate acknowledgement in any subsequent edition of this publication.

Text
Extract in Interpretation 1 on page 19 from *The Feudal Kingdom of England 1042–1216*, Longman, (Frank Barlow 1999) p.292, with permission from Taylor and Francis; Extract in Interpretation 2 on page 21 from *King John England's Evil King?*, Tempus Publishing Ltd (Ralph V. Turner 2005) p.91,The History Press with permission; Extract in Interpretation 1 on page 25 from *Crown and Country A History of England Through Monarchy*, Harperpress (Starkey,D 2010) pp.198-9, reprinted by permission of HarperCollins Publishers Ltd; © 2010 Starkey,D; Extract in Interpretation 2 on page 28 from *Domesday Book to Magna Carta 1087–1216*, Oxford University Press (Poole, AL 1993) p.422, by permission of Oxford University Press, USA; Extract in Interpretation 1 on page 36 from *Lionheart and Lackland, King Richard, King John and the Wars of Conquest*, Jonathan Cape, (McLynn, F 2006) p.120, with permission from The Random House Group; Extract in Interpretation 1 on page 45 from *Lionheart and Lackland, King Richard, King John and the Wars of Conquest*, Jonathan Cape,(McLynn, F 2006) p.121, with permission from The Random House Group; Extract in Interpretation 1 on page 51 from *Holy Warriors. A modern history of the Crusades*, Routledge (Phillips, J 2014) p.153, with permission from The Random House Group; Extract in Interpretation 1 on page 57 from *Lionheart and Lackland, King Richard, King John and the Wars of Conquest*, Jonathan Cape, (McLynn, F 2006) p.232, with permission from The Random House Group; Extract in Interpretation 1 on page 71 from *King John: England's Evil King?*, Tempus Publishing (Turner, RV 2005) p.118, The History Press with permission; Extract in Interpretation 1 on page 75 from *King John*, Yale University Press (Warren, WL 1997) p.179, with permission; Extract in Interpretation 1 on page 83 from *King John. Treachery, tyranny and the road to Magna Carta*, Hutchinson (Morris, M 2015) p.259–60, with permission from The Random House Group; Extract on page 86 from *The Plantagenets; The Kings who made England*, Harperpress (Jones, D. 2012) pp216–7, © 2012, Jones, D., reprinted by permission of HarperCollins Publishers Ltd and Capel & Land Ltd; Extract on page 89 from The Penguin History of Britain: The Struggle for Mastery:1066–1284 by David Carpenter (Penguin Press, 2003) pp.301–2, Copyright © David Carpenter, 2003.